DEMYSTIFYING LOVE

To George
SBBrown

DEMYSTIFYING LOVE

PLAIN TALK FOR THE MENTAL HEALTH PROFESSIONAL

STEPHEN B. LEVINE

Routledge
Taylor & Francis Group
New York   London

Routledge is an imprint of the
Taylor & Francis Group, an informa business

Routledge
Taylor & Francis Group
270 Madison Avenue
New York, NY 10016

Routledge
Taylor & Francis Group
2 Park Square
Milton Park, Abingdon
Oxon OX14 4RN

Printed in the United States of America on acid-free paper
10 9 8 7 6 5 4 3 2 1

International Standard Book Number-10: 0-415-95599-8 (Hardcover)
International Standard Book Number-13: 978-0-415-95599-7 (Hardcover)

Library of Congress Cataloging-in-Publication Data

Levine, Stephen B., 1942-
  Demystifying love : plain talk for the mental health professional / Stephen B. Levine.
    p. cm.
  Includes index.
  ISBN 0-415-95599-8 (hb : alk. paper)
  1. Marital psychotherapy. 2. Love. 3. Sex. 4. Interpersonal relations. 5. Psychology. I. Title.
  [DNLM: 1. Love. 2. Sexual Behavior. 3. Interpersonal Relations. 4. Couples Therapy. 5. Marital Therapy.   BF 575.L8 L665d 2007]

  RC488.5.L48 2006
  616.89'156--dc22
                        2006020262

Visit the Taylor & Francis Web site at
http://www.taylorandfrancis.com

and the Routledge Web site at
http://www.routledgementalhealth.com

To our three beautiful beloved grandchildren—

Lucy Violet, Dahlia Eve, and Sally Bea

Contents

Preface

When I set out to write a book on love, I imagined a short, relevant volume to be read by mental health professionals of all stripes. Sex was to assume a decidedly secondary role, although paradoxically, I hoped to explain much about sex by not emphasizing it. During my psychiatric residency there was a similar approach to clinical sexuality. Sex was taught with the assumption that it could be sufficiently illuminated by discussing the larger context in which it occurred. In 1970, the dominant context was thought to be the individual's early life development, particularly during the period when the Oedipus complex was believed to be influential. Since 1970, depending on the bias of the writer, sex continues to be understood as a product of various dominant contexts — for example, biology, interpersonal relationship, individual adult psychology, social class, and culture. I reject the notion of one context being consistently dominant. I assume that all sexual behavior — normal and abnormal,

partnered or solitary — is simultaneously constructed of biological, individual psychological, interpersonal, and cultural elements. Love, like sex, must have contributions from the same
four elements. It has not been easy for me to write about the
subject. Early in my career, it did not seem to be a topic for professionals to address, although I knew even then that love was
important to good sex. It wasn't until I was in my early 50s that I
felt I was mature enough to explore this province of popular culture. It was only at that point that I began to dare to talk about
love in lectures and write about the subject.

The haunting subject of love has been lurking around my
office for decades. I suspect that it lurks around other mental
health professionals' practices as well, whether they have a general adult practice, one that focuses on sexual difficulties, or a
practice that primarily treats children and adolescents. Every
chapter in this book was written with my colleagues in mind.
The first five chapters of *Demystifying Love* are idea-centered. I
avoided giving clinical vignettes because I assumed that mental health professionals would have no trouble relating to the
ideas. I presumed that their minds would be flooded with case
examples from their own clinical practices as well as memories
from their own private lives. I employed case examples in the
final three chapters because I felt examples were necessary to
illustrate the more controversial concepts concerning the private circumstances of infidelity and the art of psychotherapy.

This book may cause some concern among those colleagues who like to classify books as belonging to a particular psychiatric ideology. I have never been interested in identifying myself with any one psychiatric school of thought. Behaviorists occasionally take me for a psychoanalyst while psychoanalysts eventually recognize me as not one of their own. I have long wanted to be able to transcend such distinctions and discuss topics in a way that would invite all to enter into the dialogue. I aspire to write without psychiatric jargon. Those who strongly identify with a psychiatric ideology may find *Demystifying Love* insufficiently grounded in their favorite theory. I expect they could add many references from their literature to the concepts discussed here. I am also certain that those in other fields — literature, philosophy, comparative religion, anthropology, sociology, music, poetry, and others — have much of value to add to my concepts of love. I apologize to those who have written about love whose articles I have missed and to those who know of wonderful treatments of the subject of which I remain unaware. There is no such thing as a complete literature review on love.

I recognize that the style of this book, its first-person voice, and its commitment to discussing underlying basic concepts, is a departure from modern scientific medical writings about psychiatric or sexual topics. In the majority of professional works, authors' writings begin with the concept of disorders — such as hypoactive sexual desire disorder or erectile disorder, and then proceed to deal with treatment techniques and results. The emphasis in these works conforms to the recent, widely accepted standard of evidence-based medicine. There is much to be learned from this approach — and much to be missed by it. I welcome high-quality empirical data but I find it shortsighted to not consider a topic if this information is lacking. I hope readers will agree that *Demystifying Love* addresses vital topics that are highly relevant to their practices and that the book will help them to:

1. Clarify the events, processes, and emotions of love in their own lives;
2. Provide the language to more efficiently address the struggles of their patients;
3. Aid in the education of their students;
4. Offer selected readings for patients who are struggling with an issue addressed in the book;
5. Conceptualize and better understand the development of many forms of acquired sexual dysfunction.

In 2002, when I assumed the position of senior editorship of *The Handbook of Clinical Sexuality for Mental Health Professionals*, I proclaimed to my wife that it was my last big project. It was to be, I justified, the capstone of my life as a psychiatric educator. I felt somewhat sheepish, therefore, when three years later I informed her of my wish to write this book. My wife, who is a model of interpersonal grace, offered little complaint as I once again retreated most evenings and weekends to read and write. Lillian also happens to be an excellent editor. *Demystifying*

Love would be harder to understand were it not for her eagle eye for the slightly wrong word, subtle redundancy, or sentence that is clear only to me. The book also benefited from the critical sensibilities of my son-in-law, Chris Gaggero, who improved the organization and style of the early chapters. My thanks also are directed to those many patients who taught me about the topics in this volume and in particular to those who gave permission for me to write about them at length.

1. The Nouns of Love

Love is a noun and a verb, a thing and an action, a concept and an organized set of behaviors, and a subject that clinicians generally avoid. This avoidance is strange to me because love seems to be vital to us at every stage of our lives. I find it impossible to think about human developmental psychology, mental health, and psychopathology without making reference to maternal love, paternal love, friendship, sibling love, love of God, and love of recreation, vocation, learning, food, or music. The range of love is vast and its processes inherent in our fundamental essence as human beings (Lewis, 1960).

This chapter and the rest of the book are about love relationships that aspire to a lasting sexual relationship, an arena in which I have spent all of my professional life. If anything that derives from my consideration of this confined topic proves applicable to the other forms and processes of love, it will be an unintended bonus.

Romantic love has been carefully studied in behavioral science for several decades (Hatfield & Rapson, 1993; Regan, 2000). Its neurophysiology has more recently begun to be examined with imaging techniques (Aron et al., 2005; Bartels & Zeki, 2000), neuroendocrine measurements, and speculations about pathway activations (Esch & Stefano, 2005). Despite these and other impressive modern works (Gilligan, 2003) and enthusiastic journalistic interpretations of them (Gottlieb, 2006; Slater, 2006), sexual love, perhaps because it is supposed to last most of a lifetime, is too complicated for the current reach of science. Science is a bit weak-kneed before love because of its intrinsic subjectivity and because so many variables seem to shape its outcomes (Lee, 1988). What follows is not the product of a scientific process of hypothesis generation and testing. It is merely the synthesis of one person's obsession informed by reading, clinical work, and personal experiences.

What Is This Thing Called Love? The Nine Nouns of Love

I can provide at least eight answers, perhaps nine, to this fundamental question, none of which is the right or most important answer. Taken together, however, the dark mystery of this elusive thing called love begins to be illuminated. Like those academics who have tried and failed, I have no hope of defining love in a succinct sentence (Watts & Stenner, 2005). Each of these meanings of love can be periodically sensed during all stages of adult life.

LOVE IS AN IDEALIZED AMBITION

Love is so intensely celebrated in culture (Jankowiak & Fisher, 1992) that few people can grow up without longing to experience its highly advertised, full-blown version. Along with this aspiration to fall in love comes the ambition to reap love's many promised long-term rewards. Here are several alternate ways to articulate the specific ambitions inherent in love (Levine, 1998):

1. Love is an ambition to attain a lasting state of interpersonal harmony that will ensure enough contentment that the person will be able to focus on other important matters such as raising healthy children, having a good job or successful career, or enjoying life.

2. Love is the ambition to live a life characterized by mutual respect, behavioral reliability, enjoyment of one another, sexual pleasure and fidelity, psychological intimacy, and a comfortable balance of individuality and couplehood.

3. Love is the ambition to find a partner who will accompany, assist, emotionally stabilize, and enrich us as we evolve, mature, and cope with life's demands.

When individuals sense they have found the right partner to attain their ambition, they experience a great and lasting excitement. They are often eager to begin a new phase of life as a couple. When they have lived for a long time with someone and feel their lives are close to ideal, they experience a sense of mental stability and say that they are deeply satisfied. What they feel about their partner and about life in general derives from these private meanings. Despite their enviable situation, most people know their situation can change.

The ambition of love has two faces: to be loved and to be able to love another. The strength of these ambitions should not be underestimated. It can persist for a very long time after a partner continues to disappoint. Optimism that tomorrow will be a better day sustains the ambition. Even when the love relationship has been declared a failure, the twin faces of the ambition often continue to operate. The ambition to love and to be loved is not readily exchanged for a lesser set of expectations — although sometimes the partner is exchanged.

LOVE IS AN ARRANGEMENT — A DEAL

All adult sexual relationships are deals — quid pro quo exchanges of hopes, expectations, and assets. The social process for arranging such a deal is called dating or courtship. During courtship, the minds of the two people are often privately preoccupied with the answers to the question, "What will this person bring to my life?" The question can be asked about many dimensions: social, economic, aesthetic, recreational, sexual, medical, time-to-death, and more.

Young people in their first relationships generally do not prefer to think in these terms. They think more romantically and are often too embarrassed to admit that they thought about the specific assets of the partner. Their embarrassment dissipates with age and the accumulation of experiences in subsequent relationships. Love as a deal can be clearly perceived after a relationship is ended by breakup, divorce, or death and the person begins with someone new. During the second (or third or fourth) time around people are often able to weigh the factors that will determine their involvement. Not only do they carefully consider potential partners' assets, they are able to discuss their analysis of the potential arrangement with friends.

When we refer to love as a deal, we mean that the person accepts the arrangement — the exchange of assets. Each person perceives what has been offered by the partner. Of course, perceptions vary in accuracy. While there can be a lot of excitement in anticipation of making a deal, once the deal is formally accepted, people often feel a celebratory degree of pleasure, interest, and sexual desire, and think that life is good. In some cultures, parents make the deal. The adolescent or adult children only court after they know who their spouse is to be. They then hope to fall in love through courtship and the early processes of marriage.

Love Is an Attachment

Once the deal has begun to be worked out, love comes to mean a bond or attachment. People weave their psyches together and begin to feel a hunger to be with the other person more. They think of themselves as belonging with and to the other. Mental couplehood begins in the minds of two individuals early in the relationship though not necessarily at the same rate or to the same extent. Sexual activities, particularly those that involve orgasm, facilitate the private sense of attachment, and the attachment induces strong motivation to attain love's ambitions.

LOVE IS A MORAL COMMITMENT

Society has a great interest in love. After the deal is made, most people seriously think about marriage and a marriage ceremony. The rituals that sanctify marriage emphasize love as a moral commitment. While the clergy may be uncertain that the ambitions of love can actually be attained on earth, they teach the couple that love is a commitment to try to realize love's grand ambitions. The charming emotions that occur in the bride and groom and their families during the ceremony are only the internal music that accompanies the public promise of two people to honor and cherish each other through all of life's vicissitudes. The ceremony officially raises the bar of expectations; the new spouses are expected to honor their vows. Whether religious or secular, the ceremony instantly restructures life and generates a new set of obligations. Love as a moral commitment begins as a strong set of obligations for a lifetime.

People vary in how seriously they take their vows. Those who are very serious will feel painful and persistent guilt when they contemplate extramarital affairs and divorce, even many years after the marriage ceremony. The moral nature of the commitment is more excruciatingly felt when unhappily married parents grapple with the agonizing dilemma between their commitment to provide their children with two live-in parents and the wish to be free of unhappiness with their partner.

LOVE IS A MANAGEMENT PROCESS

While a couple's love exists in the mind of community ("They are a couple") and between the two attached adults as they relate publicly and privately in ways unique to couples, the most important place that love exists is in the privacy of each partner's mind.

Many of the positive and, particularly, the negative mental processes involved in loving another person must remain private from the partner. Under ordinary circumstances, we wisely do not share too much of our anger and disappointment about our partner. We intuitively realize that our partner needs the illusion that we do not struggle to love them. It is ironic that both partners tend to believe that it is not a trying struggle to love them, even though each is quite aware how often he or she struggles to love the partner. If our partners knew how much we struggled to contain our anger, disappointment, and regret over the deal we made, they would worry too much and fear the devastating impact of abandonment. We protect them.

Love as a management process is the practical day-to-day work of love. The usual immediate goals of this work are to remain prudent about what one says, to remain diplomatic about how one says it, to maintain perspective about the bigger things in one's life, and to prevent the partner from realizing what is actually transpiring within one's mind. Absolute honesty sounds good as a rule, but its interpretation has to be refined in order to not create interpersonal chaos. A husband's and a wife's marriage are two separate subjective states — his marriage and her marriage, each of which exists in the privacy of the person's own mental world.

Love is good self-management in relationship to the beloved. Much of adult life is spent with an awareness of the gap between our private sense of ideal love and our actual experience of our self and our partner in a relationship. The gap is a source of existential distress and, like all subjective distress, is buffered by an array of competing life demands ("I have children to raise"), defense mechanisms ("I keep telling myself that no partner is ideal"), and self-management techniques ("Take a deep breath and focus on your work!"). When the buffering system works, one's love relationship, while not continuously or completely harmonious, is good enough. The private mental struggle to maintain cooperative, kind behaviors exists in all people, even the happily married.

Love Is a Force of Nature

Love is a force of nature that creates a unity out of two individuals. At a certain time in life it casts our fates together, organizes reproduction, and remains vital to our adult growth and development and to the maturation of our children. This love is a skeleton that supports the sexual and nonsexual processes of our lives (Lear, 1990). It is not unlike the forces that organize reproduction in other animals. It can be studied both in terms of an individual's biologic processes and in terms of how collections of individuals behave (Crews, 1998). We humans, after all, have a great deal in common with each other. This force of nature acts upon us without a constant awareness of its presence. It is most pleasingly discussed at the beginning of relationships when people are happily amazed at the transformations in their lives that their new arrangement has brought about. But it can also be seen at the other end of the life cycle when people stay together because they have always been together, even though all the forces that brought them together have long since vanished. Older people often recognize that their partner is now an inextricable part of themselves and that they can never be psychologically free of the partner. Nature — the underlying biological force that brought them together socially — gave them culturally approved tasks that kept them together, and now having slowly attenuated their capacities, has had its way with them.

LOVE IS A TRANSIENT EMOTIONAL STATE

Love is not *a* feeling but a combination of two, and sometimes three or more feelings. The basic two are pleasure and interest. The third more variable feeling is sexual arousal. When I declare that I love the book I am reading, you can assume I feel pleasure and interest in it. When I sincerely state that I feel love for a person I may mean that I sometimes have sexual inclinations as well.

In order to understand love as a transient emotional state rather than a feeling, we must understand that the words *feeling* and *emotion* are *not* synonyms. A feeling is a simple experience of sadness, anger, disappointment, aversion, pleasure, or interest. An emotion is built from feelings but is more complex and consists of two or more simultaneous feelings. Feelings and emotions alert us to the meanings of events and processes within our relationships. They are our first warning system for the changes in our external and interpersonal environment.

Two separate patterns explain emotions. First, emotions exist because events typically create more than one feeling. Anything important to us typically creates an array of feelings. When a woman, for instance, learns that her newly beloved thinks about her in the same terms and declares his wish to marry her, her feelings might consist of pleasure to the point of joy, interest to the point of fascination, pride in being highly valued, gratitude, sexual arousal, and awe. Yes, she may be described as having the feeling of happiness, but this simple summary does not capture the separate feelings that she is experiencing, their fluctuating intensities, or their individual time courses.

Second, emotion is created because we humans have feelings about our feelings. Consider this example: A child of a certain age can experience envy. But, when a child is taught that it is wrong to feel envy, the subsequent experience of envy may evoke anxiety from the guilt of feeling something of which a parent disapproves. If the parent is watching while envy occurs, the child may experience shame as well. In this child, an initial simple feeling of envy has become an emotion comprised of envy, anxiety, guilt, and possibly shame. All of us can experience the simple feeling of envy. The emotion of envy, however, varies among us based on our attitude toward envy. Your envy may be an unencumbered feeling while mine can be a complex guilt- and anxiety-provoking array.

Here is a second example of how family and culture create emotion out of simple feeling. A religious middle-aged man averts his gaze when he sees an attractive woman, feels guilty and anxious, and tries to redirect his thoughts to his wife. He explains that this is the proper way of handling his sinful response to another woman. His mere aesthetic appreciation of another woman — a simple feeling of pleasure from someone who is visually pleasing — has become a complex emotional process.

The emotions of love are particularly complicated. Feeling intense pleasure and interest in a potential new partner quickly stimulates some internal reaction to this incipient love. It may stimulate apprehension, eagerness, or guilt, for instance, depending on the circumstances of the person's past or current life. When one person contemplates saying "I love you" to another, anxiety appears. The speaker often feels danger because he or she realizes it will have an important meaning to the listener. Sincere first declarations of love are very anxious moments. They inform the listener that important transformations have already occurred in the speaker. How will the listener respond? Pleasure and interest in the partner at that moment are often overshadowed by trembling fear.

Sexual interest and arousal are often associated with the intense pleasure and interest in a new partner. The sexual arousal continuum varies from slight genital tumescence to profound, preoccupying bodywide sexual arousal (Levine, 2003b). Since "I love you" can create sexual arousal in the listener, the phrase can be used when the primary pleasure and interest in the person is the anticipation of sex. The meanings and motives for expressing love change all the time. When a person says to us, "I love you," we have to discern both its meaning and motive. Sometimes it means only, "I want to have sex." A genuinely felt "I love you" expressed immediately after sex may reflect an intense psychological pleasure experienced during the previous moments. But such statements may be made out of politeness rather than being genuine.

Most people do not understand the difference between a feeling and an emotion. As a result, they may spend years anxiously waiting to experience the *feeling* of love. Privately, they are uncertain what love is, yet they assume others experience it. They may be tempted to fake love and mislead their partners about their degree of pleasure and interest in them. Although it may initially be shocking to learn that love is not a feeling, it can be liberating to understand the ordinary complexity of love. *Love* is the label we give to a range of transient emotional experiences. Love is always complicated by past, present, and future considerations.

LOVE IS AN ILLUSION

We want to think positively about love. We want to believe in it as a concept. We want to assume that we are loved by our partner. We want to think that we love our partners. In order to maintain these beliefs, at times we need to create certain distortions or illusions for both ourselves and for our partners. Love as an illusion refers to the fact that we create love by internal private processes, maintain it by prudent diplomatic dishonesty, and can lose it for our partner without the partner knowing it. We can courageously face the fact that the processes of love require defensive distortions of a person's feelings, thoughts, and perceptions in order to remain in an intimate relationship. *Defense* is the psychiatric term for an illusion. As individuals gain experience, many can look back and see that many of their assumptions about love were self-serving illusions. Some dismiss their entire relationship with "What was I thinking?" They usually don't literally mean that they never experienced any transient emotions of love for the partner, they mean that now they can perceive that they created illusions so as not to admit to themselves the depth of their disappointment with their partner or themselves during the relationship.

Love as an illusion does not mean that there is no such thing as love or that all felt love is an illusion. It only means that self-perceptions as loving and as beloved can prove to be inaccurate. It also means that society, through its educational and religious institutions, through its celebrations of love in song, and through its academic discourses on the topics, fosters simplistic notions about love that encourage us to behave as though we all know what it is.

LOVE AS A STOP SIGN

This ninth meaning of love is a first cousin to love as an illusion. The stop sign is visible to clinicians and others as well. While many people state that they love their partners, they are baffled, tongue-tied, or stumped to explain themselves if asked "Why?" While this can be simply an unwillingness to answer the question, the motive for the stop sign is often an unwillingness to think about the question: The stop sign is a defense against self-discovery. The statement, "I don't want to pursue the subject further!" protects the person from confronting the illusory aspects of his or her love. The word we use when we don't want to examine this arena of ourselves is *love*. Love, the stop sign, ends the inquiry.

Example 1

Lover A: I love you.

Lover B: Why do you love me?

Lover A: I don't know, I just do!

Example 2

Doctor: Why do you put up with that behavior from your spouse?

Patient: Because I love him!

Doctor: What does that mean?

Patient: I don't know.

Example 3

Patient (crying): She's using crack again, she ignores our children, she got pregnant last year during her long visit with her parents and had an abortion without telling me, and now she is running around with her drug dealer. She simply cries every time I mention how long it has been since we were together sexually. Everyone says I should divorce her.

Doctor: And why do you not?

Patient: I still love her. (Sobbing increases)

Doctor: What does that mean?

Patient: I have no idea…. I feel we could be so good together… I still vividly remember the day when I was 11 and my father left us with his suitcase in hand. He saw me crying and said he would be back soon. I did not hear from him for three years.

Our motives for entering a particular love relationship and staying in it are intensely private matters. Much of what clinicians assume to be unconscious in this regard may be a mixture of unconscious and quite conscious but private awareness. The patient may think of these motives as the darker side of love — that is, the social, material, future economic, or psychological considerations. In any particular conversation, the person may see fit to hide these motives because the clinician is not yet trusted with such personal information. Thus, "I love my partner" is a stop sign, a functional part, conscious or unconscious, of the eighth meaning of love. It says, "Allow me to maintain my illusions please."

Lurking behind the stop sign may be the belief that the person's love for his or her partner is not genuine. The person may not understand that love is ordinarily part illusion. The stop sign may be a reflection that he or she does not understand the nature of love.

Final Thoughts

I have a suggestion for how to use this chapter: eavesdrop. The next few times you hear or read the word *love*, professionally or privately, see if you can discern which of the following noun meanings of love is being invoked. Is it love: the ambition; the deal; the attachment; the commitment; the management process; the force of nature; the emotions; the illusion; the stop sign, or something else? Then consider whether you think the speaker or writer demonstrates any awareness of the range of possibilities of meanings of this word.

Finally, I want to acknowledge a limitation of the metaphor of love as a noun. While the noun title headings are static sounding, my descriptions of each of the nine nouns are quite dynamic. The nouns have an ongoing, ever-changing impact on our mental lives. The nouns of love create the verbs of love. After we have considered the processes or the verbs of love in Chapter 2, I hope we will agree that love is a series of things and behaviors across the life cycle. Love is not a set of nouns *or* verbs, it is both, and each needs the other to be understood.

2. The Verbs of Love

Love is a dynamic process of change. At its beginnings, love is rich with marvelous possibilities. As its processes unfold, disappointments crush many individuals and eventually the couple. In our consideration of the verbs of love, we aspire to illuminate the processes of love.

Love Evolves

If a couple begins their relationship with intense pleasure, interest, and sexual desire and lives a long life together, every dimension of their love will inevitably evolve. The most predictable aspect of the evolution is the dissipation of sexual passion. This typically occurs in three sequences. The first decline is usually complete well before two years into the relationship (Tennov, 1979). Sexual frequency often is reduced to about 50% during this period and loses its sweet urgency. The frequency of sex, even mutually orgasmic sex, then is prototypically relatively stable for about two decades (Dennerstein, Smith, Morse, & Burger, 1994).

It gradually begins its further and final descent in midlife. At the onset, the ideal couple experiences consummate love consisting of passion (intense sexual desire), friendship (psychological intimacy), and commitment to be together exclusively forever (Sternberg, 1988). If still together at the end of the life cycle, the same couple's love will be companionate. It will likely contain a more deeply intertwined, wordless knowledge of each other and a more profound functional caretaking commitment than during earlier stages. What it will lack is sexual energy. The couple may occasionally still have some form of sex together, not because either needs to as in the past, but because one or both wants to. The time it takes to evolve from consummate to companionate love varies enormously from couple to couple. Many forces — major physical illness, major and minor mental illness, disappointment in the partner, problems with children, infidelity, bankruptcy — can hasten the onset of the companionate phase.

Falling in Love

The process of falling in love requires only one person. The one-person experience occurs far more often than is acknowledged. One-person love stories begin with personal dissatisfaction with one's life. Then something attractive is perceived in another person. This perception triggers an imaginative excursion about what might be. These fantasies are accompanied by mental excitement. This process temporarily rearranges our psyches. Occasionally, a one-sided love is never directly acknowledged but is sublimated into many years of devotion or friendship. Most often, however, the spell of infatuation is broken by actually dealing with the person and discovering that the initial impression was wrong or that the person displays a negative characteristic that is more powerful than the attractive one. The infatuated person then experiences disappointment, embarrassment, and self-castigation about being so foolish.

In contrast to the private humiliation of such infatuations, the well-known two-person phenomenon of falling in love is endlessly charming. The usual meaning of "falling in love" is the beginning of requited love. Fictional love stories are often about overcoming the external obstacles to love, but in real life, the issue is more often about overcoming internal obstacles to making a loving arrangement (de Botton, 1993).

THE DEFENSES

Falling in love involves the defenses of denial and idealization. These mechanisms for creating illusions are more or less required during this intrapsychic rearrangement. In the relatively brief process of falling in love, many of those around us feel that we have exaggerated the capacities and minimized the limitations of the newly loved. They often privately say skeptical things to one another about our psychological state: We are in denial about the capacities and traits of the person; we are idealizing the new person; we are being naïve because we fail to appreciate the implications for the future of what we do see.

Excitement and Skepticism

A new love relationship holds much potential, generates new experiences, requires new sensibilities, and will propel the person to a new level of social and psychological existence. Throughout both the ancient and the modern world, new love has had the reputation for being transformative (Ackerman, 1994). People who fall in love are often keenly aware of the need for something different in their lives. Some think that we fall in love out of this need for psychological or social change (Aron & Aron, 1996). Denial and idealization enable individuals to break down the boundaries that exist between them and their partner, to create a new personal identity as a couple. The employment of these defenses is motivated by the private hope of personal improvement. "I will be a better person and my life will be better with this person."

Everyone newly in love faces the same issue: "Which is correct, my hope-generated judgment or my skepticism?" This central issue reverberates in the minds of the newly fallen as they recurrently ask themselves two questions, "Am I being realistic? Will I be damaged?" Personal skepticism is often quelled, however, by the new psychological intimacy with the partner. Although we may deny, idealize, and appear naive about some aspects of the person, we have a view of the partner that the external skeptics do not have. Some of the perceptions that derive from this knowledge may be more correct and trustworthy than the observations of our friends and family — we hope.

The trepidation that a person feels upon entering a new state of love is largely explained by risks inherent in making a deal with another person. Some of the trepidation may be based upon an activation of anxiety left over from anxious infant and toddler attachments (Bowlby, 1989; Roisman, Collins, Sroufe, & Egeland, 2005). Exploration and analysis of the trepidation, however, is made difficult because having a new person in one's life generates a great deal of excitement. One is finally close to realizing the grand cultural ambitions of love.

When people explain their new happy emotional state they often employ dramatic words such as *earthshaking, trance, beguiling, amazed, exhilarated*, or they speak of exultation and rapture. When falling in love is sudden in onset, volcanic in intensity, and a bit irrational, it is sensed as occurring from outside the self. People grasp the metaphor that they have been struck by Cupid's arrow. Plato was mindful of the myriad of intense feelings that accompany falling in love (Plato, 1956). He explained them in this way: the basic protohuman form contained both male and female elements. These elements become separated at birth. When we fall in love we think that we have finally located our long-missing other half. All of these feelings of excitement make thinking clearly about the partner a difficult challenge. The happiness of this state has not deterred skeptics. Freud described falling in love as the only time it was normal to be psychotic. Samuel Johnson quipped that this mental state was a disease best cured by marriage.

FALLING IN LOVE'S ESSENCE

The essential process of falling in love is an act of imagination. Imagination creates the images of a highly desirable life with a particular person. We imagine attaining the cultural ideals of love. Falling in love is the beginning of the process of creating an idealized internal image of the partner. This internal image, which psychoanalysts call an internal object, will play an important role throughout the life of the relationship, sustaining commitment during difficult times.

Being-in-Love

After a person has fallen in love, during the subsequent courtship, the person has to privately decide whether the deal is a good one, to discern whether the partner thinks similarly, and to propose the arrangement. The full intensity of early love, its emotional crescendo, is reached when we are reassured that something comparable to our internal upheaval over the newly loved is occurring within the other; that is, we are becoming our beloved's beloved. Singer has labeled this marvelous phase as "being-in-love" (Singer, 1984). Since falling in love requires a personal act of imagination, being-in-love requires the accurate perception of the other's creative burst. The two phases are commonly confused with one another. When the important interpersonal task of the falling-in-love stage has been accomplished and the partner is in a similar state, the couple, now in the being-in-love state, begins to take on life together.

Being in love typically lasts much longer than falling in love, but it too, relatively quickly loses its early dominating intensity. It is gradually replaced by a calmer, far less tumultuous period of contentment during which life is increasingly preoccupied with realistic external concerns. Even so, we experience our new partner as idealized, not merely in the sense that traits are overestimated or failings are not perceived, but in the sense that one is finally on the way to realizing the grand ambition to love and be loved. We will do everything possible to stay on this high road.

It is here, in the uncertain, recently turbulent processes of two people ascertaining whether they are simultaneously in love and resigning themselves to bear the inherent risks, that their willingness to behave sexually often reaches a pinnacle. Sex is wanted, rehearsed mentally, and is experienced with a deliciousness that is long recalled. These early shared sexual pleasures further enhance the sense of the union's rightness and deepen the couple's attachment to one another. During this passionate phase people have difficulty resisting the fallacy that their good sex is a sign that everything else must be fine. While the term *passionate love* conveys the intense sexual desire inherent in early love (Baumeister & Bratslavsky, 1999), the desire that is actually passionately stimulated is a desire to be happy, to be understood, to be in agreement about important things, to guard the well-being of the partner, and to live an exalted life (Alberoni, 1983).

Bergner has explained why sex is so valued during this phase of love (Bergner, 2005). He emphasizes that sex communicates to each lover that he or she is appreciated, admired, accepted, and respected. The sexual behaviors make clear to the partners that each is included in the other's inner life, that they understand each other, and that they have become exclusive to one another. Each lover's status is enhanced by the lovemaking; each feels affirmed. These pleasures, which are conceptually separate from the physical pleasures of sex, derive from the affirmation of being loved. Bergner calls the lovemaking an accreditation ceremony.

If the couple is able to withstand the mundane challenges of beginning to function as a couple in society, and many do not (Sprecher, 1994), they enter into the greatest challenge for a couple — remaining a couple who privately feel satisfied being together.

Staying in Love

Staying in love is easier said than done. Its processes probably involve an unknown, most likely large number of intermittent steps through the life cycle. I assume that they are, in fact, none other than the ordinary nonsexual developmental challenges of adulthood, which originally were outlined by Erikson (1963). Each step has the potential to subtly or not so subtly restructure life, add new roles, preserve or impair sexual function, and deepen one's appreciation of the self and partner. The degree of mastery of these steps shapes the highly individual evolution of our love. The study of the evolution of love is the study of adult maturation. The individual variations in how people master these many challenges account for the unpredictability of love.

Here are just a few ordinary examples that challenge a couple's ability to stay in love: having a first child, having a second child, being promoted, dealing with the decline of one's parents, accumulating excessive debts, menopause, and personal or spousal illness. I assume that all people are in a continual state of maturational change. These changes involve our intimate relationships, our feelings about our partners, and our behaviors within those relationships. Like all other maturational processes, they are apparent in their effects but not in their mechanisms. Some people naively expect to be loved unconditionally — that is, regardless of their behavior or capacities. Adult relationships are highly conditional. We are constantly being evaluated by their partners.

APPRAISAL AND BESTOWAL

Staying in love is the product of two ongoing, hidden mental activities: the assessment of the partner's behaviors, particularly the person's recurrent patterns (appraisal) and the granting of cooperation (bestowal) (Singer, 1984). It is not correct that our partners simply and constantly feel love for us. Partners notice our behaviors, give them meanings, and depending on what they perceive, feel pleasure, admiration, disappointment, or anger. When our behaviors create positive feelings, our partners are more cooperative, affectionate, and enjoy us. These behaviors shore up our idealized internal image as loved. I think of them as putting money in a bank. As positive experiences accumulate under diverse conditions over time, our partners treat us as though we possess good character.

Although we do not constantly feel pleasure and interest in our partners, we allow them to think that we do. They make erroneous assumptions because we are committed to behaving in a kind, helpful fashion. Our idealized image of our partner enables us to act in a loving way because we do feel loving toward the partner's image — if not to the actual partner sulking upstairs.

Continuing negative appraisals of our behavior and character interfere with our partners' pleasure from and interest in us — that is, their ability to love us. They rob our partners of their sexual interest in us and attenuate their commitment to love us by eroding their internal image of us as being worthy of respect. Our partners then find it difficult to bestow affection and cooperation. Despite the fact that some people remain relatively quiet as they accumulate negative appraisals of their partners, the process is nonetheless momentous. At a certain point, these negative appraisals come to dominate a person's thinking about the partner. This may then trigger new mysterious anxiety, panic, guilt, or depression as the person confronts the question, "Now, what am I to do?" For a while, it seems that people prefer to think of their new symptoms as a mystery. They may take some psychotropic medication. But eventually they come to realize that it is only in their best interests to keep the source of their feelings from their spouse. Some wait for a better day with the partner and seek a calmer acceptance of their partner's capacities and style. Others, however, privately decide to terminate the relationship.

DEFENSES ARE NECESSARY

We need illusions about our partners' capacities, attributes, and attitudes toward us to minimize our disappointment with them. We routinely rationalize away some of our disappointment by telling ourselves to be *realistic* about what can be expected from any partner. If the reality of our relationship is not close to our ideal, we try to move toward the ideal in the privacy of our minds. And there we may repeatedly emphasize what is close to the ideal — she is a good cook, he is a good father — rather than focus on what is not: "I wish she could enjoy sports with me"; "I wish he were not so withdrawn and asocial." There are good reasons to be so *unrealistic* about our partners: after all, they have been chosen to accompany, assist, stabilize, and enrich us as we grow.

The hidden processes of maturation change our understanding of ourselves, our partners, and of the ideals of love. As we understand ourselves better, we may cease to be as critical of the partner for traits that we possess. Our private sense of our partner changes many times. We eventually lose some of our illusions about them. We inevitably see them more clearly as we recognize recurring patterns of their behavior, we better realize their strengths and their limitations, and we judge their integrity and trustworthiness. Maturation sooner or later dissipates somewhat our private struggle to love and to be loved. We surrender to the knowledge that we love in our idiosyncratic ways and so do our imperfect partners.

THE VERBS OF LOVE

The phrase *the verbs of love* has two separate meanings. The first one encompasses the processes of love — falling, being, and staying-in-love — that rearrange our psyches and our behaviors. The second meaning involves the highly individual styles with which we go through these processes. Individuals express their ambitions to love, their felt responsibilities to the partner, their felt emotions, and their defenses in a unique manner. Even when both partners in a couple understand the nouns of love in the same manner, they translate these nouns into behavior in different ways. The verbs of love are even more individualistic than the nouns. Being in and staying in love are often matters of defining and accepting the compatibilities and incompatibilities of each person's style.

COMPETENCE IN A LOVE RELATIONSHIP

There must be a set of behaviors that enables an individual to form an enduring union that is satisfying to both partners (Donnellan, Larsen-Rife, & Conger, 2005). These behaviors could be present in one or both spouses. These relationship competencies might account for marital longevity and self-reports of marital happiness. Marriage is so complex and varied that we should not expect that any one therapist or researcher's synthesis will serve as the last word on competence in love relationships. Nonetheless, such competence seems to be characterized by a consistent pattern in which hostility is absent, and there is the presence of warmth, respect, support, and a willingness to engage with the partner to solve mundane problems (Gottman, 1998). The sense of friendship prevails even in the face of disagreement.

PREDICTORS

The predictors of staying in love have been empirically studied over many years by Gottman (1998). He and his colleagues suggest that successful couples possess an ability to repair their relationship when things inevitably go wrong. These couples found mechanisms to deescalate moments of negativity through expressions of positive feelings about each other. This deescalation and evident positive regard occurred even though the couples had some unsolvable problems. Women's soft presentation of a problem or complaint and men's willingness to stay involved in the discussion were strongly predictive of marital stability and happiness. The other empirically validated predictor of stability was men's ability to accept influence from their wives. Humor helped maintain an environment of positive emotion. Successful couples recognized the need to stay connected in the face of their disagreements. Their stability and happiness did not depend upon their ability to resolve their problems. The key to staying in love was their ability to maintain a dialogue about them. Gottman and his colleagues' longitudinal work emphasized that these attributes did not change in successful marriages after the birth of the first child. The husband was still emotionally there. Their work has thus far only focused on the predictors of happiness and stability in the early years of marriage (Gottman & Krokoff, 1989). Staying in love, of course, is a lifelong challenge.

Psychoanalysts assume that the root of most dysfunction is in early life intrafamilial processes (Kernberg, 1995). The work of Gottman and his colleagues and the developmental tradition come together when couples who withdraw from one another surround their relationship with negative affect. They thereby escalate their conflicts to create a less than ideal environment for children. Poor marital skills or relationship incompetence expose children to personal developmental disruptions due to the high tension, high-decibel environment in which they live. But, in addition, distressed parents are often preoccupied and relatively unavailable to minister to the children's needs (Gottman & Katz, 1989). This can occur prior to the psychological, social, physical, and economic disruptions induced by divorce. The challenge of staying in love, therefore, is highly relevant to the entire family.

THE STRUGGLE WITHIN THE SELF TO STAY BALANCED

Staying in love is in large part the result of what happens in the privacy of one's conscious mind; perspective is the key. Largely unknown to partners, but apparent to individual therapists who spend time with unhappy spouses, many dramatic conflicts are enjoined in the patients' minds. These include the struggles of appraisal vs. bestowal; pleasure vs. resentment; attractions to others vs. moral constraints; initial vs. alternative meanings for the same partner behaviors; self-interest vs. partner interest; self-interest vs. child interest. The privacy of the individual's own mind is the usual location for the work of love. When a person says, "I love you" to a spouse he or she may mean "believe me, I'm really working on it."

THREE ADDITIONAL CONCEPTS ABOUT STAYING IN LOVE

1. *Genuineness.* Fromm suggested that long-term love requires the remeeting of two people at the point of their emotional genuineness (Fromm, 1954). As all people face expected and unexpected challenges in life, the important differences among us may be our abilities to face our individual and joint challenges together as a supportive, sympathetic team. By genuineness Fromm meant sharing our thinking, emotions, and the pleasure or pain from the consequences of our decisions. Today most of us mental health professionals assume that such genuineness begins with the ability to be honest with oneself. When we meet people who cannot face their own inner world of emotions and recognize that they possess conflicting motivations, we should wonder whether these characteristics make them more difficult for their partners to love. Genuineness requires the ability to be psy-

chologically intimate with another. Intimacy provides pleasure and interest to the partner. Genuineness breeds psychological intimacy, which in turn breeds love and sexual desire.

2. *Overcoming narcissism.* It is important that each person develop the ability to put him- or herself second at times. Overcoming narcissism means increasing devotion to the partner, couple, and family — putting the needs of the partner, the couple, or the children ahead of one's own (Levine, 1998). Partners notice the degree to which this is accomplished; we can more easily bestow cooperation when our partner's self-interest is put aside. It also adds to the loving internal image of the partner — that is, it puts that psychic money in one's private mental bank.

3. *Negotiation.* While some people are autocratic, dictatorial, or feel entitled to make the decisions for the couple, even this unbalanced circumstance is the result of some form of prior negotiation. The partner who does not like confrontation, disagreement, or directly representing personal interests decides to go along and find spheres of activity that the other person is not interested in controlling. In many couples, however, many decisions are discussed, options weighed, and each person's wishes are taken into account. Compromises are deliberately found that please each person. Love as a commitment conveys the responsibility to try to satisfy the wishes and needs

of the partner. To get one's needs met, people have to make them clear in a calm, direct fashion. Everything from meals to sex, from what to spend money on to which family to visit during the next holiday, from what style of clothing a child should be dressed in to which couple to go out with, is in some way negotiated in a long-term relationship. Those who are more skillful at diplomacy and seek a position that satisfies both people, have an advantage in this realm. Negotiation begins in courtship when one seeks basic compatibility of interests, ambitions, and values. It continues throughout life as two people inevitably discover their differences in taste, temperament, energy, interests, organization, and so forth.

Partners prove to be great challenges when they either escalate or withdraw in the face of interpersonal conflict; cannot be genuine; cannot be depended upon to put themselves first with their spouse and children; feel entitled to make all the decisions and expect others to accommodate their decisions. Their partners may come to love only through commitment and its attendant work. They may state that they love their partner even though their love lacks pleasure and sexual interest. Subjectively they come to feel that their love is empty and they long for a fresh start or are preoccupied with their memories of the good days together: Many of them divorce.

3. Professional Humility and the Erotic Transference

The first two chapters have provided a conceptual background for understanding patients' stories about their lives. Regardless of the initial complaints, patients' stories soon become focused on their personal relationships. The details vary enormously, but disappointments in how patients are treated in love and how they feel about their partners are common themes.

This background knowledge of love does not urge me to attempt a new nosology of love problems. Nor does it dictate one particular strategy for improving marital relationships or efficiently increasing an individual's or a couple's competence in relationship behavior. I feel profoundly humble in attempting to reverse the destructive course of a couple's marriage. And yet, the evolution of my awareness of these nouns and verbs seems to have propelled me to a greater efficiency in helping those who consult me with their concerns about their love or sexual lives.

How the Nouns and Verbs of Love May Help

Most conspicuously, the nouns and verbs of love have helped me to understand more clearly what it is that people are saying. I have new words and phrases to more precisely describe my patients' situations to them. Patients respond positively to being understood in this way. Implicit in this understanding is that they are not alone in their struggles to love and be loved. My employment of these concepts has often created a positive transference.

The concepts have helped me in a more subtle way by causing me to think more directly about how people stay in love. It has spurred me to commit myself to some guidelines for staying in love (Levine, 1998) and to tailor these guidelines to couples' life stories. I talk about, for instance, overcoming self-interest, being appraised by one's partner at all times, and how to rephrase a position in a diplomatic manner. Understanding the diverse meanings and processes of love has led me to realize that, though disguised as psychotherapy, much of what I do is educational. I have become more active in the therapy hour. I listen for fewer minutes per session before I speak. I assert what I believe they need to understand to transcend their current dilemma; that is, I act as though I believe relationship competence can be conceptualized, learned, practiced, and can quickly generate a modest pleasure in being together. I believe that other therapists might benefit from my idiosyncratic synthesis of this ever complex domain of staying in love.

Practical Applications

The patient or couple and I realize, even if we never state it directly, that they must be doing something wrong in their relationship. *They are failing to stay in love.* I assume they are seeking my assistance in finding a new understanding of the process, new ways of obtaining their partner's positive appraisal, and some inspiration to counter their demoralization. In order to quickly achieve these aims, I often find myself selecting one or more of the following ideas to introduce to them late in the first session or in the second one. After I have listened to them explain how they see the problem, it is their turn to listen to me.

THEY HAVE TWO SEPARATE MARRIAGES

In every marriage there are two subjective marriages — one for each partner. Within each person's private subjective marriage the person perceives the partner's behavior, appraises it as worthy of respect or disappointing, as loving or as selfish, as adding to the positive regard of the internal image of the partner, or as remaking that image in a negative manner.

EACH PARTNER IS A LEGITIMATE MEANING MAKER

Each partner not only finds and attributes meanings to all that the spouse does, but has a cohesive sense of the spouse's psychology as well as of his or her own psychology.

It Rarely Makes Sense to Argue Over Whose Meanings Are Correct

Rather, it is vital to recognize the separateness of each person's meanings and to become interested in the partner's meanings. This is *not* a matter of agreeing with these meanings; it is only a matter of understanding the ordinary inevitability of a separate sense of meanings. The couple can now stop arguing, speaking louder, threatening the other person — the usual poor strategies for winning an argument — and begin to practice discerning each other's meanings.

Every Argument Is About a Specific Issue

The couple must quickly identify the issue that has provoked their interpersonal tension and seek to define what their conflicting positions actually are on the issue. Each person can then provide, while being listened to without much interruption, the meanings imbedded in his or her position.

Disagreements Do Not Have to Be Settled Today

Once the issue and the conflicting positions are clarified, the couple feels a bit better. They can then wait and see how they feel tomorrow about the same issue. Tomorrow often brings slight changes in emotions and positions on the issue. Compromise is often then more possible in such a way that both parties are reasonably pleased. Pleasing both parties then may become a new goal in disputes. The issue is not over until both people's views have been seriously dealt with.

THE PARTNER'S PERSONALITY IS OFTEN
THE ISSUE BEHIND THE ISSUE

In a long-term relationship, appraisal and bestowal of affection and cooperation are increasingly based on awareness of the partner's character traits. By "character" we mean the habitual patterns, capacities, or incapacities of the partner. The work of marriage is often the process of accommodation to the partner's character. Over time, the partner sees the spouse's character more clearly. It is easy to help a distressed couple articulate what it is about the partner that is so problematic or disappointing to him or her. When I initially hear the story of a problematic incident in the couple's life, I find myself listening for the characteristic behaviors of the person in the story, because it is not the incident in itself but what is typical about the incident that brings the couple to me.

THE PARTNER'S PERSONALITY SHOULD BE DISCUSSED
PRIMARILY AS THE SPOUSE EXPERIENCES IT

The volatile topic of the partner's personality should not be discussed as "You are…." Rather, it can be discussed as, "How I experience you, how I think about you." In this way, the actual subject of the sentence is the speaker and not the partner. It encourages silent attentive listening without stimulating a vengeful need to criticize the spouse who just spoke.

THE VOLATILE FIRST SESSIONS

I find it necessary to state three rules for a happy marriage that should never be broken (of course, they have just broken them in front of me).

1. No name calling; no ad hominem characterizations as bitch, asshole, bastard, cunt.

2. No threats of abandonment such as suddenly floating the idea of a separation or divorce, or abruptly leaving home without apparent destination, because these are usually strategies to win the argument through frightening the partner into submission.

3. No needless assaults on the spouse's vulnerabilities. Within several months of knowing a person well, his or her private sense of vulnerability becomes obvious. During disagreements, because of frustration and anger, partners may "go for the jugular." This is a big mistake because it establishes the partner as cruel and is very difficult to pass over. Learning about the partner's jugular carries with it a commitment to protect the partner from slashes at the throat.

THERE IS NO COMPREHENSIVE NOSOLOGY OF LOVE PATHOLOGIES

Informally, the pathologies of love are those patterns that prevent or limit the processes of falling in love, being in love, and staying in love. These are quite diverse and range from the obvious to the subtle. Individuals of almost any adult age can fall in love. Staying in love can be a 60-year-plus challenge. Studies of love tend to be model based. The models are typically tested on college students. The love stories of people in the second half of life tend to be ignored.

The absence of a nosology means that the academic underpinnings of the subject have been relatively ignored in recent decades. The problems of love, however, frequently pose important issues for all clinicians, not just marital or sexual therapists. Here are a dozen recurring examples:

1. What are we supposed to do with those physically or emotionally symptomatic patients whose symptoms reflect their unhappily married state?

2. How are we to respond to the individual who needs assistance with his or her inability to get along — that is, who lacks relationship skills?

3. What are we to do with the person who seeks help for a psychogenic sexual dysfunction because of its impact on the relationship?

4. What are we to do about patients who develop an erotic transference to us?

5. What are we to do about the appearance of seemingly forbidden personal erotic fantasies about a patient?

6. What should we teach our trainees about the subjects of love, sex, and their relationship to one another?

7. In our well-intentioned prescriptions of psychotropic medications, are we inadvertently injuring some patients' ability to love and to be loved by causing sexual symptoms?

8. What impact does the patient's Axis I diagnosis currently have on his or her current love and family relationships?

9. What role has the patient's Axis II diagnosis had on his or her love relationship, and what bearing does it have on the Axis I diagnosis?

10. What impact do the patient's sexual interests or the patient's spouse's sexual interests have on the patient's presenting problems?

11. How do I recognize when the patient's presenting problem — anxiety, depression, sexual dysfunction, and so forth — has no relevance to the subject of love?

12. What are we to say to those who are incompetent as a spouse but pathologically jealous when separation is a possibility?

Such questions remind me that issues involving love are more central to the work of the mental health professional than is usually assumed. When I recall one of the ambitions of love — to find a partner who will accompany, assist, emotionally stabilize, and enrich us as we evolve, mature, and cope with life's demands

— I come to understand a broader series of patients' complaints as related to disappointment in their current relationship.

LOVEMAKING?

Sex between two people is often glibly referred to as lovemaking, even though the arrangements that people make for sex do not necessarily depend upon the emotions of love. After several years together a couple can readily distinguish between making love — acting upon the feelings of eager arousal which in turn stemmed from an appreciation of the partner — and just having sex because it is Saturday or the partner is crabby. Sexual behavior occurs for numerous reasons during the course of a relationship, even though we tend to lump them all under the heading of lovemaking.

The concept of lovemaking as an accreditation ceremony (Bergner, 2005) helps to illuminate the infamous dynamics of some late adolescent or young adult male sexual ambitions. Bergner explains that some men (occasionally women) devote themselves to the pleasures of having a woman fall in love with them. They are unwilling or not yet ready to allow the process to proceed in a conventional fashion. They do not fall in love with the woman. They never had any intention of doing so. What they are seeking besides the mere opportunity for sexual intercourse are the many affirmations that her loving them provides. They get accredited by the woman who expects to be accredited in return. The latter does not happen and she feels victimized when she realizes it. Such Don Juans are admired by inexperienced men and hated by women.

It does not matter much if clinicians refer to these phenomena as immaturity, insincerity, lack of genuineness, Don Juanism, or narcissistic exploitation (Kernberg, 1995). In every era writers recognize certain dangers early in the processes of love (de Botton, 1993). Freud wrote about the phenomenon of those who could not unite the two aspects of the sexual instinct, affection and sexual pleasure, in one person. This was his explanation a century ago for why some men and women could have pleasurable sex and could affectionately love as long as each occurred with a separate person (Freud, 1905/1953).

Since the early 1990s, clinicians have witnessed the appearance of a large number of male patients with syndromes variously known as sexual addiction, sexual compulsivity, or hypersexuality (Cooper & Marcus, 2003). Often middle-aged by the time they seek assistance, they have already put enormous strains on their love relationships, if they have been able to establish them (Bergner, 2002), and have usually created so much chaos within the family that divorce is a distinct possibility during treatment.

These well-known love pathologies cannot be specifically delineated within *DSM-IV-TR* (American Psychiatric Association, 2000). The best that we can do is to accurately diagnose other aspects of the person's life and wonder what role the definable disorders have played in how they love and are loved.

LOVE AND PROFESSIONAL HUMILITY

Mental health professionals, of course, want to be seen as and to feel competent in their roles. Certainly our patients want to believe that we are highly competent at what we do. But whether it is about giving medications to psychiatric patients (Insel, 2006; Lieberman et al., 2005; Rush et al., 2006), providing a PDE-5i to man with erectile dysfunction (Levine, 2006), or working with a couple on their recurring conflicts, our competence cannot be based simply on the stability of our results. In the conceptual sphere of love, where most practitioners have not dwelled, it is soon clear with many couples that we do not have easy answers to their love problems. I find this to be a great advantage. It enables me to remain a humble student of the forces that shape our lives. The clinical reality of love problems can keep us all professionally humble.

I am deeply distrustful of mental health professionals who find their work easy, their results excellent, who know how to resolve complex matters quickly, or whose theory explains it all. Our outcome data and our individual experiences do not warrant the slippery claims routinely made in the marketplace of self-help books. Professional humility is the beginning of clinical wisdom. It is also a means of preventing those occasional tragic circumstances in which a mental health professional and his or her patient become sexually involved with one another.

Mishandling of Erotic Transference

A mature clinician is expected to have a working understanding of the matters discussed in the first two chapters.

SOCIETY HAS EXPECTATIONS OF US

We are assumed to understand and respect the potential of a person to fall in love, to know that each person possesses a powerful imaginary wish-fulfilling capacity, and to grasp the fact that loving another is often a response to a significant social or psychological problem. These are the conceptual tools that society expects us to have in order to help patients who have an erotic transference to us. They are what we use to help patients understand what is occurring within them. This knowledge keeps therapy serious and patient focused, and prevents the therapist from believing the patient's narcissistically gratifying distortions about the doctor. Even though the patient has come to think of the doctor as very attractive — that is, powerful, omniscient, emotionally stabilizing, and the object of sexual desire — the doctor knows this is a defense against facing a painful past, a painful present, or both. It is easier for the patient to long for the therapist than talk about something about which he or she feels helpless. The therapist is paid to help patients to move through this process. The irony, however, is that although society (state boards, professional societies, courts, and the media) expect clinicians to know about these mechanisms, trainees in the mental health profession are not taught them.

"I FELL IN LOVE WITH HER!"

Sometimes a mental health professional offers a very poor explanation for his sexual behavior with the patient. He conveys a sense of helplessness when he explains, "I fell in love with her." When he says this, he does not yet comprehend how this appears to more sophisticated colleagues. Some people really understand the nature of the internal processes of love and think that all professionals do as well. Colleagues who may personally feel sympathetic with the tragic therapist perceive him as naïve, unaware of his own narcissistic gratification, and incompetent in maintaining the correct focus on the patient's motives during the therapy. If his colleagues don't believe his explanation, however, they will simply see him as a lying rooster in a henhouse; one who takes sexual advantage of dependent, needy women. So, either the doctor is naïve — that is, unaware of how his unhappiness spilled into and ruined his patient's therapy — or he is viewed as a predatory, psychopathic liar. This is not a happy differential. "I fell in love with the patient" is not a sentence I like to hear, particularly from a mental health professional.

The patient's erotic transference can be used for the patient's benefit as long as there is no possibility of the doctor agreeing to enter into the patient's world as a sexual or life partner (Gabbard, 1998). Marriage is no longer a way to legitimize having had sex with one's patient. The doctor must respect the patient's frustrations in life and believe in the patient's creative capacities to find solutions for them. We must grasp the concept of sublimation. When the doctor agrees to be the sexual solution for the patient's frustration, outsiders will view his behavior as using the patient for his purposes. An ethics committee will accuse him of violating the principles of autonomy, honesty, beneficence, and nonmalfeasance (American Psychiatric Association, Ethics Committee, 2005; Roberts & Dyer, 2004). The state board will ignore the facts that the patient brought up the idea in the first place, was relentless in pursuit of the doctor, and eagerly consented to all sexual behaviors.

I have been through these tragic circumstances with physicians, psychiatrists, and psychologists a number of times (Levine & Risen, 2006). It is difficult not to be sympathetic to them in the privacy of my office because I know that they did not understand the concepts about love that I consider to be basic to our work. I also grasp that they were not taught about this in sufficient depth in graduate or postgraduate training. They share their emotions with me and tell me about the boundary violation from their viewpoint. I participate in their anxieties about their license, their social and marital losses, and their depressions. It is just that the public viewpoint simplifies doctor–patient sex as a serious, often career-ending violation of the social contract of being a professional and prefers to think of the doctor as a bad person.

MY SOLUTION

Colleagues on state boards know that respectful boundaries between patient and doctor are a reflection of the professional's intuitive understanding of the power of love and a conscious commitment to not victimize the patient. Unfortunately, many of us in our profession do not quickly enough understand the processes of love when we are the object of desire. My solution is that mental health professionals should learn about love in detail. We should cease our conceptual avoidance of the word and study both the nouns and verbs of love at the same time we study professional ethics.

4. The Path to Love
Psychological Intimacy

The topics of love, psychological intimacy, and desire intertwine in such important ways that it is somewhat misleading to discuss them separately. I have chosen to do so, nonetheless, because each topic is important on its own and may have different uses for the reader. This chapter, for instance, has proven to be an excellent introduction to those beginning to learn about the clinical interview. It is even more relevant to those who are starting a career as a psychotherapist. For these two groups, it can be used much before the topics of love and desire usefully fit into their sequence of learning. The experienced clinician, however, should have little difficulty integrating this trio of topics into a useful whole.

An Introduction to Psychological Intimacy

Sexual and psychological intimacies are often confused. What they have in common is that each involves contact with the inner or private self. The contact can be physical, psychological, or both.

INTIMACY'S USEFUL AMBIGUITY

Psychological intimacy implies familiarity and understanding, and sometimes affection and love. The word *intimacy* when used alone refers to sexual behavior without explicitly naming it.

PRIVACY AND EVOLVING INTIMACY RULES

The closeness that both kinds of intimacy create usually occurs in a private setting. Although the setting is often a place like a bedroom or a restaurant, setting can also refer to a context — a type of relationship that exists between two people. Society passes judgments on the appropriateness of the context. Social definitions of appropriateness, however, such as in the matter of a couple's premarital sexual behavior, are changeable. For example, American society is moving in the direction of, but is still not absolutely certain that sexual intimacies between graduate students and their professors are inappropriate. Since the early 1990s, however, sexual contact between undergraduate students and professors has been treated as unethical. Since the mid-1980s, our society has developed certainty about sexual intimacies within psychotherapy; they are now so unacceptable that they are often harshly punished. We have become wary of two-way psychological intimacies between junior and senior high school students and their teachers because we suspect that can be a prelude to the older or more powerful person taking sexual advantage of the younger and less powerful one.

MOST CONVERSATIONS ARE NOT PSYCHOLOGICALLY INTIMATE

Extensive psychological intimacies are avoided in the vast majority of social contexts. Behavior is more polite, functional, and superficial than personally significant or touching. Most social contexts, as a result, are likely to prove tiresome when a person is seeking psychological intimacy. Psychological intimacies are not boring; at the very least they are interesting, and, they can be enthralling. People who are only skilled at small talk or frequently speak of a third person whom the listener does not know, risk losing the listener's interest far more quickly than those who initiate psychologically intimate conversations.

Psychological Intimacy and the Mental Health Professions

The employment of psychological intimacy in our work as mental health professionals is so basic to what we do that we generate it automatically, reflexively, without much awareness. Most of us have forgotten that we once had to learn how to foster psychological intimacy in others and to respond to it in such a way that maintained its powerful benefits. Society expects the medical profession to quickly form psychologically intimate relationships with patients in order to assess, diagnose, and begin to offer patients relief from their difficulties. This basic professional form of psychological intimacy is easy to attain since patients expect us to listen to their story. All we have to do is not too egregiously interfere with their telling of it. The more difficult aspects of our one-sided intimacies occur as we continue to meet with our patients. They then have to retell the same story with more details, tell additional stories, and speak more spontaneously without the same conviction that they possessed at the first meeting about what was relevant to their problem. After our initial evaluation, we are expected to speak more. Our words are expected to be helpful, to relieve suffering, or to change the relationship of the patient to him- or herself or to the world. This is the difficult part, even for experienced mental health professionals.

Therapy is to be accomplished without the relationship falling into a two-sided psychological intimacy. Friends, lovers, close siblings, and spouses have two-sided psychological intimacies. These intimacies result from a shared emotional experience, typically from conversation alone. Both one- and two-sided psychological intimacies involve sharing intense emotional experiences. In our one-way professional intimacies, the patient has an intense emotional experience; we have a far more objective, cognitive experience with much less private emotional arousal.

SOMEONE HAS TO SPEAK FOR PSYCHOLOGICAL INTIMACY TO BLOSSOM

Psychological intimacy begins with a person's ability to share her or his inner experiences with another (Levine,

2003a). This deceptively simple sounding capacity actually rests upon three separate abilities: (1) the capacity to know what one feels and thinks; (2) the willingness to explain it to another; and (3) the skill to express the feelings and the ideas with words. The absence of any of these three abilities limits the chance of establishing and maintaining psychological intimacy. For instance, some people do not recognize what they feel, even when their feelings are intense. The best they can do is to say that they are "upset" before or after they behave in some problematic manner. Others do not trust anyone enough to share their inner experiences. Still others, like a tourist in a country whose language is unfamiliar, are limited by their language skills; they know what they are experiencing but they cannot explain it.

The crucial first step toward psychological intimacy is the sharing by one person of something from within the inner self. What is shared need not be elegantly said, lofty in its content, or unusual in any way; it just needs to be from the inner experience of the self — from the continual monologue of the speaker's self-consciousness, from the speaker's subjectivity. Even if the speaker is able to bring these three capacities to the situation, psychological intimacy will not occur unless the listener in turn can provide an adequate response.

The Listener Must Perform Well
for Intimacy to Blossom

The listener has to respond to the speaker in a manner that conveys:

1. An uncritical acceptance of what is being said;
2. An awareness of the importance of the moment for the speaker;
3. A grasp of what is being said;
4. A sense of privilege that he or she is present to hear what the speaker has to say.

We mental health professionals should be excellent listeners. We should so well understand these ideas that they are automatically incorporated into our professional activities. While professionals have subtle variations from one to another in how well we listen, when a therapist and a patient are in conversation, we want the patient's lack of self-awareness, unwillingness to share, or inability to express ideas and feelings to be the only obstacles to psychological intimacy.

Inadequate listeners prevent psychological intimacies. They make negative comments such as, "You shouldn't feel that way!" They fail to acknowledge the significance of what is being said to them by impatiently remarking, "Can't this wait? Don't you see how busy I am?" They may miss the point of the speaker's words. Or they too quickly return to the speaker role. Such failures prevent friendships from forming, people from becoming lovers, and spouses from maintaining their sense of connection.

What Is Professional Psychological Intimacy?

When the patient and the professional perform their respected tasks reasonably well, psychological intimacy occurs. The two people connect; they share a transient, rarefied pleasure. The shared pleasure is the intimacy. Here are its components.

The patient's pleasure is in large part solace — a form of peace or contentment that results from sharing the inner self, being listened to with interest, and being comprehended. Solace is the response to being seen, known, understood, and accepted. Intimacy, however, also brings the sense of excitement, energy, and an uplifting of mood. Overall, the experience of intimacy for the patient may be stunning. This flow of emotion may, in and of itself, immediately offer both hope and relief. This response creates the basis for the idea that we sell psychological intimacy for a living. People in emotional distress need and want the restoration of hope. Our uninterrupted attention to grasping the patient's story can transiently improve the patient's mood, energy, and outlook. The professional's pleasure results from hearing about the speaker's inner experiences. The professional is trusted enough to be told, competent enough to have enabled the telling, perceptive enough to accurately summarize the speaker's story, and wise enough to respond without censure. These quieter pleasures of intimacy for the clinician should be routine. Veteran clinicians become jaded by their experience with intimacy. But new clinicians learning our skills are often themselves stunned and excited by what they have facilitated. They, too, feel a new contentment.

I have just defined intimacy in my way. Others frequently employ the term, but in my reading experience, it is either without a specific definition or it is something that is attained in countless ways (Scheinkman, 2005; Wynne, 1986).

What Is Two-Sided Psychological Intimacy?

Let's imagine two people are having a successful date. Both individuals take turns being a speaker and listener and each is reasonably good at the roles. As a result of their conversation, each person feels some degree of pleasure — solace, contentment, or excitement. And each feels the quieter purr of being trusted with personal revelations that are not generally heard in public arenas. Each experiences the ordinary emotions of the good speaker and the good listener discussed above. In this context, however, both parties are apt to interpret their private feelings and sensations as the earliest glimmer of love. If the next date is also a psychologically intimate one, there can be a dramatic intensification of their pleasure and interest in one another.

Initially, the two individuals' understanding of the context of their relationship largely determines their behavioral response to speaking and listening. Not only does society set its standards for context, but the individuals involved limit what takes place between them, and what they allow themselves to feel in response to speaking and listening. The difference between a professional and a social psychological intimacy is not always in what people actually feel, but what they allow themselves to think and do about what they have experienced.

THE IMMEDIATE CONSEQUENCES OF TWO-SIDED PSYCHOLOGICAL INTIMACY

As revealing two-way conversations occur, powerful internal processes are stimulated within each speaker/listener.

The Bond

Most outside observers can recognize that the reciprocal sharing of the inner monologue with a person who receives it well creates a bond between the speaker and listener. Thereafter, each regards the other differently; the two people are together in a new way. They glance at each differently; touch each other differently; laugh together differently; and can continue to readily discuss other aspects of their private selves. Yet much more occurs within the two people than can be observed from outside of them. Within both the speaker and the listener, there is a feeling of attachment, a loss of the usual social indifference, a vision of the person as special. Intimate conversations ignite new processes. The listener becomes internalized within the speaker and, since both are performing each role, they internalize one another. "She is *my* new friend!" "She is *my* patient!" Internalization, the invisible bond, has other predictable consequences. These include:

1. Imagining the person when she or he is not present;
2. Inventing conversations with the person;
3. Preoccupation with the person's physical attributes;
4. Anticipation of the next opportunity to be together, and missing the person's presence;
5. Dreaming about the person;
6. Thoughts about that person as a sex partner.

The intensity of these consequences varies from relationship to relationship. When two-sided psychological intimacy occurs, we begin to weave the person into our selves. Our new intimate partner is not only reacted to as a unique individual, but she or he stimulates thoughts, feelings, and worries that we previously experienced in relationship to others. This often complicates two-sided psychological intimacies.

Reviewing these ordinary consequences of early two-way psychologically intimate conversations helps us to understand why many people interpret as love the pleasure they feel from the conversations and the interest they discover in listening to and speaking with their friend. They may downplay this a bit by referring to their "chemistry," but they privately mean love. We do not have to agree or disagree because it is clear that they are bearing the intrapsychic consequences of psychological intimacy.

Consequences of Professional Psychological Intimacy

The mental health professions have recognized for almost a century that something akin to this happens in our offices during some of our work with patients. We designate this process as transference. The intensity of the therapist's concentrated interest in, wish to understand, and desire to help the patient evokes transference reactions. Sometimes we try to use a patient's transference to us to educate the person about past experiences. Ideally, such therapy helps patients to peel off their transferences to significant others so that they can react to their partner on his or her own merits rather than according to how the patient was treated years ago by someone else. Most modern therapies do not quickly focus on transference; they are more problem focused. But even while the focused conversation between patient and therapist is occurring, their bond may be deepening, the patient's pleasure in being listened to and understood is becoming a form of emotional sustenance upon which many patients quickly come to depend. Psychological intimacy is a form of nurturance, support, and connection which can come to be highly valued by the patient. The patient experiences pleasure in seeing the therapist, has a great interest in the therapist, and feels an important attachment. In other settings, such private responses would be called love.

ALL PSYCHOLOGICAL INTIMACIES CAN
PROVOKE EROTICIZATION

The amount of time required to imagine the person as a sex partner — that is, the speed of the eroticization provoked by intimacy — is modified by at least seven factors: age, sex, sexual orientation, social status, purpose in talking together, the nature of other emotional commitments, and the person's attitudes toward private sexual phenomena. If the pair consists of a comparably aged, socially eligible heterosexual man and woman, the eroticization triggered by sharing of some aspects of their inner selves can occur with lightning speed — in both of them. Similarly, for a pair of gay men or lesbian women, eroticization can occur in a flash. The stimulation of the erotic imagination may never occur, take a long time to occur, or occur only in a fleeting disguised way, depending on how these seven factors line up. Many adult psychological intimacies do not lead to eroticization. Friendships are valued because they afford an opportunity to share the self without the intrapsychic burden of eroticization. The specific emotional experiences that occur as a result of intimate conversations are usually guarded with extreme care. They can be exceedingly exciting both generally and erotically. Some individuals who are new to intimate conversations may have fear about their intense responses to their new friend. They feel so excited that they wonder if they are losing their mind. The power of the excitement of a new psychological intimacy with a friend can be strikingly similar to the power of the imaginative burst of falling in love. We think it is normal and cute when 10-year-old boys and girls form new inseparable friendships and physically hang on each other endlessly.

Clarice, age 10: "Mom, I just fell in love with Sara."
Mother: "That is nice, dear."

College students living in dorms, meeting new people, sharing their affective excitement about their increasingly emancipated lives and their intellectual growth have a lot both to talk about and to listen to others about. There are many transient sexual relationships spawned in these settings and there are some highly personal, inhibited homoerotic excitations as well. A person has to be able to tolerate the stimulation that a new friendship induces. Most young people do not recognize the similarity between a new friendship and falling into a romantic love. Some individuals are unnerved by their internal responses to new friendship and spend their lives aspiring to emotional closeness but subverting it.

THE LONG-TERM EFFECTS OF PSYCHOLOGICAL INTIMACY

Without repetition of the solace/pleasure experience, the positive consequences of intimacy prove to be short-lived. In order for two-sided psychological intimacy to fully blossom, periodic sharing of aspects of the inner self is required. There are good reasons to continue to share over time. Reattaining psychological intimacy provides a sense of security about the relationship.

It calms the individuals by allowing them to be seen, known, accepted, understood, and treated as unique. This is the stuff of friendship, good parenting, and being and staying in love. Long-term sexual relationships are often characterized by what seems to be a premature loss of sexual behavior. What typically precedes this is the loss of psychological intimacy. It is important to consider psychological intimacy as an aphrodisiac.

While most friendships are not bothered by mutual eroticization, most sexual partners expect to be dear friends. Dear friendships and good lovers do some of the same things for us: They stabilize us — they make us feel secure, happy, and good about ourselves. When psychological intimacies disappear from previously important relationships — no matter whether they involve spouses, lovers, friends, or a parent–child unit — various anxiety, depressive, or somatic symptoms may appear.

Psychological Intimacy Is a Potential

One-sided psychological intimacies are common between children and their parents, patients and health care professionals, clients and lawyers or accountants, and advice-seekers and clergy. Two-sided psychological intimacies are the basis of friendships, good familial relationships among older children and parents, and sexual love relationships. Psychological intimacy's potential depends on the degree of self-disclosure and nuance of attention and understanding. No two intimacies are quite alike; each relationship is uniquely rich or poor in its possibilities. People with more than one intimate friendship are not necessarily intimate with each friend about the same aspects of their lives. People who have had several lovers recognize that there were differences in the degree of psychological intimacy attained, the personal material discussed, and the lovers' responses to private revelations. It may be only a potential but it is quite a vital one.

PSYCHOLOGICAL INTIMACY AND GENDER

A generation ago, a process began of compelling theoretical work about the essential psychological styles of girls and women (Gilligan, 1993). Normal women came to be understood as typically requiring more frequent psychologically intimate experiences — with each other, with children, with lovers, with husbands — than do men. Women complain more than men to therapists about the lack of psychological intimacy in their relationships to men (Gilligan, 1993; Jordan, 1989). Men are more typically patterned to more autonomous operational patterns. They have trouble understanding why women complain about their lack of communicating, why they say their marriages do not contain enough intimacy. Today it is broadly recognized that healthy women organize their lives to a far greater degree around relationships — to friends, family, lovers, children, and spouses — than do healthy men. Women expect themselves to be relational, to gravitate to connection, and to personally evaluate their successes in terms of psychologically intimate relationships and responsiveness to other person's lives. Men tend to think of themselves as successful more often in terms of the creation of a unique, self-sufficient wage-earning self. These gross generalizations about the gender differences leave room for the scientifically verified observation that no one psychological trait is the exclusive province of either gender. Men prosper in intimate relationships as well as women do.

RELATIONSHIP BETWEEN PSYCHOLOGICAL AND SEXUAL INTIMACY

Psychological intimacy lays the groundwork for select people to become lovers. It is often the trigger to falling in love. Once a couple become lovers, the sexual behavior creates a further sense of knowing each other. People experience each other's nakedness and their behaviors during sexual arousal. Sex allows them to know a person in ways that few others can ever know them. In the early phases of a relationship — the being-in-love stage — sexual and psychological intimacy creates a positive feedback loop: one form of intimacy stimulates the other form.

For the long haul, it is the ready reattainment of psychological intimacy that enables the couple to make love again and again over decades, to shed their inhibitions during lovemaking, and to eventually discover the limits of their sexual potential with one other.

In any sexual relationship, over time it becomes increasingly difficult to behave sexually together without psychological intimacy. Lovers may quickly discover that talking, communicating, or sharing how one thinks and feels about a relevant matter increases their willingness to behave sexually. Psychological intimacy, however, requires each partner to set aside time to reestablish it when the sense of disconnection or distance is felt by either of them. This can be a formidable problem for those who do not intuitively understand these ideas, cannot provide the speaking or listening skills, are chronically overwhelmed by other external demands, or who originally could manage only a meager intimacy. As a result, the sexual potential of psychological intimacy is not realized — sexual desire is severely limited by the absence of psychological intimacy.

5. Sexual Desire
Simplicity and Complexity

Sexual Desire Is a Concept

In one very short sentence, here is my working definition of sexual desire: Sexual desire is the sum of the forces that lean us toward and away from sexual behavior. The definition is couched in a mathematical metaphor for a reason. This human longing is the result of the interaction of positive and negative shaping influences. These influences, which are often present simultaneously, are the implied pluses and minuses in the mathematical formula.

On the surface, sexual desire does not seem this complex. It appears to be a single mental force, an energy. Many professionals think of desire as being either normally present or abnormally absent. They expect young people to have it, people in a pleasing courtship to be preoccupied with it, and happily married people to possess it for most of their lives. They are less certain about older people, however. About 100 years ago, the medical world adopted a sophisticated-sounding professional word for this force: *libido.* Today many still think that libido is merely a Latinate synonym for sexual desire. Freud used the term for a hypothetical sexual instinct that organized much of life's activities beginning in early childhood (Freud, 1905).

Today, sexual desire is our culture's term for the *cause* of the following subjective phenomena: sexual fantasies, heightened awareness of another person's attractiveness, and genital and breast sensations. Similarly, it is the term for what propels these behavioral phenomena: planning for solitary or partner sex, initiating sexual behavior, or responding receptively to a partner's initiation.

While it is tempting to believe that these varied manifestations are produced by a single appetite (Kaplan, 1977), this assumption ironically makes the quest to understand sexual lives more difficult. As mental health professionals have learned in other arenas, the mind possesses the capacity to camouflage how it operates. Our minds create the illusion that sexual desire is a simple phenomenon, but embracing this idea only confuses us.

All sexual lives quickly become complicated by conflict, paradox, contradiction, and moral dilemma. It does not take very long, for example, for a sexually naïve 12-year-old girl who discovers that she can bring about voluptuous clitoral sensations to realize that masturbation may not be a morally acceptable act. Like the relationship between a feeling and an emotion described in Chapter 1, she reacts to her act of masturbation with feelings. Her desire to feel those wonderful sensations again may be happily repeated or guiltily, anxiously put off or compromised. Masturbation is about as simple as sex ever gets and yet it becomes convoluted for many young people (Tolman, 2002). Recognizing the ordinariness of the complexity of desire helps us to realize how difficult it is for many people to grow up to become fulfilled, civilized sexual human beings.

The Endowment and the Dynamic Spectra of Sexual Desire

We are not all created equally when it comes to how much sexual desire we possess over the life cycle.

ENDOWMENT

We vary considerably in terms of the frequency and intensity of spontaneous and reactive genital sensations, erotic sensitivity to others, preoccupation with sexual fantasies, time spent planning for sexual behavior, and comfort with *not* behaving sexually. A woman, for example, may feel the need for sex daily, every three days, for three days before every period, or about twice a month. Those with high sex drives arrange for sexual behavior frequently and feel more calm and able to concentrate on other matters after orgasm. People with low sex drives may have spontaneous sexual feelings but they can readily ignore them without feeling irritability and distraction. They can go for long periods of time without sexual behavior and remain comfortable. Our varied endowments come into view by considering any similarly aged group of people. A majority fall in between the polar extremes of low and high sex drive, although they may have periods of their lives when they occupy one pole or another. Both men and women can be found at each pole (Langstrom & Hanson, 2006). The endowment spectrum can confuse clinicians when they need to diagnose patients. Labels such as *hypoactive sexual desire disorder* and *sexual addiction* are readily applied to people who normally exist on the poles. Knowing about this spectrum does not help us discern where to draw the line between normality and abnormality on either the high or the low end of desire endowments.

Dynamic Desire

During even relatively brief periods of mental and interpersonal stability — for instance, when aged 30 and happily married — sexual desire can shift from intensely positive through neutral to intensely negative. In the positive range, people have thoughts such as "I'm so horny!" They also initiate sex. In the neutral to disinclination range, people grant sexual behavior only because of the other person's interest. They are receptive to sex. Negative desires range from the prospect of sex being unappealing to the more intense, "I can't stand the thought of sex tonight!" The ordinary dynamic spectrum of sexual desire's intensity looks something like this:

Aversion↔Disinclination↔Indifference↔
Interest↔Need↔Passion (or Lust)

The dynamic spectrum can be seen in those with high, moderate, and low endowments. It can even be seen in some depressed people, whom psychiatric texts usually characterize as having a decreased libido, because they can experience the full range of sexual desire manifestations depending on what is currently happening in their lives.

THE SLOW EVOLUTION OF SEXUAL DESIRE

The trend for sexual desire over the life cycle is downward. Younger people often report that they spend more time on the right side of the dynamic spectrum while older people often report that they more or less reside to the left of the middle. They feel desire less frequently and less intensely than their personal memories of their young adulthood lives. As a result, youthful and older age sexual behaviors have different characteristics (Butler, 1975). Youthful sex can be sudden, intense, impatient, naïve, and a bit clumsy; older age sex can be quieter, more skillful, less mysterious, and often biologically limited. Between these eras, many people explain their decrement in desire by invoking partner familiarity, alienation, or preoccupation with nonsexual matters. These are powerful considerations, but so is the biological weakening of sexual desire. This is most apparent in the 50s when most people are having sex less often. When we look at populations, the quieting of sexual desire as we move through the life cycle appears to be biological in origin. When we clinically consider an individual's life, however, interpersonal or psychological determinants seem to be more apparent than the effect of aging.

Sexual Desire Consists of Three Components

In any individual, at any time, sexual desire is created by the interplay of biological, psychological, and cultural forces.

1. *Drive, the biological force.* The biological component of desire has an unmistakable basis in anatomy and neuroendocrine physiology. While this is known with scientific certainty, the specific factors that account for different endowments have not been clarified. Neither have the immediate precursors to feeling spontaneously "horny."

2. *Motivation, the psychological component.* The psychological component translates into the degree of willingness a person has to enter into sexual behavior with a particular partner at a moment in time. Motivation to have sex is influenced by emotional states such as joy or sorrow; interpersonal states such as mutual affection, admiration, disagreement, or disrespect; duration of the relationship and cognitive states such as moral disapproval or religious uncertainty about having sex for personal pleasure.

3. *Values, the cultural component.* Families, schools, religious institutions, political processes, regional influences, historical influences, and economic forces can shape a person's sexual desire and behaviors. These influences begin in childhood, and, once present, can change as individuals are exposed to new ideas as they mature. Values serve an evaluative mental function. The mind screens all personal sexual behaviors with two questions: Is the behavior normal or abnormal? Is it morally acceptable or unacceptable? The answer to the first question reflects an understanding of the world while the answer to the second one reflects the person's conscience. Values augment or diminish sexual desire by affecting our willingness to engage in sexual behaviors. Values are camouflaged as motivation.

Cultural forces are insidious. They affect us in ways that we do not initially perceive. History is instructive about this. In the 19th century, when masturbation was widely viewed as a public health menace, in regions where the populace knew that the devil resided in the "flesh," and when women were expected to provide sexual pleasure but not experience it, the chances of growing up at ease with sexual expression were limited. Different concepts of sexual normality and morality existed in the past (Engelhardt, 1974).

Time	Drive	Motivation	Values	Desire
Today	3+	1+	0	4
Next week	1+	1+	-1	1
Next month	0	4+	3+	7

Figure 5.1 A mathematical illustration of the components of sexual desire and their fluctuation.

THE MATHEMATICAL METAPHOR

The shaping of sexual desire by the interplay of biological drive, willingness to bring one's body to a particular partner for sexual expression, and thoughts about the normality and the morality of the specific behaviors varies from sexual episode to episode. At any given moment, the valence of each of the three components can be a plus or a minus. Consider these possibilities in Figure 5.1.

What Else Clinicians Need to Know About Sexual Desire

Knowing that sexual desire is the sum of the forces that move us toward and away from sexual behavior is not enough for clinicians. We need to be able to recognize and deal with four variables that routinely influence the positive and negative intensities of the three components of sexual desire.

SOCIAL SITUATION

Consider these evolving social circumstances of adult life: Unattached, committed, engaged, happily married, wanting to be pregnant, pregnant, new parents, unhappily married, having an affair, divorcing, divorced, widowed, dating, recommitted, remarried. These situations subtly determine whether people think that their fluctuating experiences of desire are a problem or not. When they seek our assistance, we too consider their social context as we try to understand their motivations to have and to avoid sex.

When young and single, we often feel an intense need to connect intimately with others as we search for an ideal life partner. We may experience ourselves as having frequent sexual drive manifestations. After that connection is firmly established and we sense that we have marched through the falling in love and being in love phases, we may celebrate our new loving bond with an exuberant frequency of sexual behaviors. Soon, however, despite the cultural expectation to continue regular and frequent sexual behavior, one or both partners' sexual desire lessens. Unless a partner wants to engage in some behavior that is sensed as abnormal or immoral, the values component of sexual desire is no longer very determinative. Sexual desire becomes a matter of fluctuating drive and motives for sex. When the couple wants to get pregnant, their sexual motivation usually increases. When we want to reaffirm our affection or commitment, convey our remorse for our past bad behavior, or reclaim our errant partner, sexual desire can again become intense. When we grieve for a partner, desire may quietly slip away only to awaken intensely when a new partner materializes.

These observations help us to realize that sexual behavior is a nonverbal means of self-expression and of interpersonal communication. Many an embarrassing sentiment — such as, I'm sorry; I missed you; I'm angry; I'm desperate; It's time to get back to normal — is carried on the wings of sexual desire. Most of these sentiments are kept private from the partner but they can also be secret from the self. Sexual desire may shift on the dynamic spectrum without the person being aware of the cause of the shift. Clinicians spend a great deal of time and energy trying to assist patients in linking their sexual desire levels to their social contexts (McCarthy, 1999).

GENDER

Gender is such an important factor in sexual desire that we might think of it as two separate subjects — male sexual desire and female sexual desire (Basson, 2000). We assume that gender organizes sexual desire both through biological and socialization processes, although no one is able to prove how much each contributes. Speaking only on average, males have more sexual drive than females from puberty on. Male drive, initiations, and aspirations for sex last longer in the life cycle and are far more reliably present (Regan & Atkins, 2006). Female sexual drive, being weaker on average, is more easily ignored by women and eradicated by social circumstances. There are many consequences of this difference in the strength, persistence, and reliability of drive. The one that is initially hardest to grasp is that sexual desire distorts women's sensibilities far less than it distorts men's sensibilities (Levine, 1999). Socrates said that he was glad that he was an old man because once his sexual fire died down, he could think more clearly.

The testes make approximately 7000µg of testosterone per day and convert 1% of it to estradiol. The ovaries generate approximately 300µg daily and convert 50% of it to estradiol (Federman, 2006). Women's desire fluctuates in response to the menstrual cycle, pregnancy, lactation, menopause, fatigue, and the ceaseless maternal roles they play. Women's motivation is highly sensitive to subtle positive and negative interpersonal contexts. Each woman defines this context within her subjectivity. Women aspire to psychological intimacy as a gateway to sex whereas men are more inclined to aspire to sexual behavior as a gateway to the sense of closeness.

Another consequence of the differences in desire plays out in most long-term monogamous unions. What begins as different sexual drive endowments in individuals becomes a private, unavoidable political matter within every relationship. Drive differences create the need for negotiation for every couple. The negotiations deal with both partners' drives and psychological intimacy needs. Many people expect to negotiate with few if any words, believing that direct references to their sexual drive manifestations are crudely improper. Inadequate negotiations may play a role in generating a couple's sexual withdrawal from one another (Clement, 2002).

Gay and lesbian couples also have to negotiate for their sexual and psychological intimacy needs. In their one-on-one politics, individual differences in desire cannot be attributed to gender per se but to individual differences.

The distinctions between drive and motivation in women of low and moderate endowments are difficult to discern and may not be important (Basson, 2001). In these women drive may have been primarily motivation. Basson has pointed out that the linear model that portrays desire as step one, arousal as step two, and orgasm as the final step does not seem to apply to most of her patients. She posits that women's sexual receptivity is motivated by numerous personal and interpersonal psychological considerations. In many marriages, women's desire for sexual behavior begins to consciously appear only after arousal has begun. Basson draws a circular model of the interplay of drive, motivation, intimacy, arousal, and orgasm. The negotiations of heterosexual couples for sex involve the clash of linear and circular patterns. Some desire disorders may be the product of a couple's poor intuitive grasp of their gender-based differences.

A number of sexologists have proposed that desire in both genders may only be early arousal (Everaerd, Laan, Both, & Van Der Velde, 2000; Meston & Frohlich, 2000). One day, rather than discuss sexual desire, all of us may speak of arousability as the essence of sexual function, and then address our clinical attention to the conditions that facilitate and prevent its appearance. If this is correct, drive manifestations may only be sponta-

neous arousals, motivation for sex may only be allowing oneself
to be aroused by the anticipation of sex. It is easier to engage in
sexual behavior from the sensations of early arousal than from
preoccupation with nonsexual matters.

Aversion↔Disinclination↔Indifference↔
Interest↔Need↔Passion (or Lust)

While the above dynamic spectrum of sexual desire applies
to men and women, a subtle difference exists at its far right end.
Women more often invoke the word passion (Person, Terestman, Myers, Goldberg, & Salvadori, 1989) and men more often
invoke lust (Stoller, 1975) to communicate this point on the
spectrum. For instance, when heterosexual men look at pictures
of naked young women or watch strip club shows, they often
find themselves in a state that they call lust. At this moment,
their desire is for more arousal. All of their worldly concerns temporarily disappear as they single-mindedly pursue this goal. Men
experience lust most easily in settings where the partner has no
personal relationship to them. Strippers have the power to create this relatively pure sexual feeling state because their behavior
says, "I exist only for your pleasure, sir!" Nothing from real life
complicates the illusory experience. The relatively pure sexual
feeling state called lust can occur in normal — that is, complicated relationships, as well. It seems to occur more often between
new lovers than spouses. In actuality, however, this state of only
wanting more arousal routinely occurs shortly before orgasm in

both sexes. It is, alas, quite transitory. The same can be said of passion; it is common but fleeting. I suspect, however, that men think of lust as relating to a body and women experience passion as relating to a body within a relationship rich with possibility. Of course, individuals of any orientation can experience the right end of the desire spectrum.

AGE

In all mammals, sexual frequency and capacity decline during the middle and older years (Schiavi, Schreiner-Engel, Mandeli, Schanzer, & Cohen, 1990). This is most readily seen among women in the dramatic increase of sexual complaints during the peri- and menopausal years (Dennerstein, Smith, Morse, & Burger, 1994) and among men in rising incidence of erectile dysfunction in the sixth decade (Feldman, Goldstein, Hatzichristou D. G., Krane R. J., & McKinlay, 1994). It is important to juxtapose women's and men's midlife sexual declines so as not to falsely encourage us to seek a solution in hormone replacement for what may be a more fundamental early aging phenomenon. Physicians used to promise women that estrogen/progesterone replacement at menopause would keep them sexually "young" (Greer, 1991). More recently, there is similar hope for a testosterone cure for women's midlife sexual decline (Shifren et al., 2000). Not only have the data on the negative effects of hormone replacement therapy for menopausal women provoked caution and skepticism about such claims (WHI Writing Group, 2002), but more recent studies of drugs intended to alleviate desire problems have had to contend with a problematically high placebo response rate (Basson, McInnes, Smith, Hodgson, & Koppiker, 2002; Goldstein, Lue, Padma-Nathan, Rosen, Speers, 1998) and the failure to demonstrate adequate long-term safety (Basson, 2006). Aging does not impact all men and women similarly, however. Some remain functional even though drive declines (Rowland, Incrocci, & Slob, 2005).

HEALTH

Both subtle and conspicuous mental and physical health problems diminish drive and motivation and sometimes create moral qualms about making love to an affected spouse (Okabe & Mishima, 2004). There are important exceptions to the rule that serious illness diminishes sexual desire. These include mania, sexual compulsivity as a response to depression, sexual abuse-induced hypersexuality, and treatment with multiple dopaminergic agents (Korpelainen, Hiltunen, & Myllyla, 1998). Nonetheless, impairments of health cause both people with an illness and their partners to think and feel differently about sex (Schover & Jensen, 1988). Such new thoughts typically diminish sexual motivation for the partner. Disease processes such as a prolactin-secreting pituitary tumor; treatments such as the SSRIs and sympathetic blocking agents may eradicate drive; and the dignity-robbing loss of social function, such as occurs with advanced multiple sclerosis, all can diminish motivation in patients *or* their partners. Physical health provides only the potential to experience sexual desire. Other life processes must stimulate and maintain desire.

WHAT STIMULATES SEXUAL DESIRE?

A list of stimuli of sexual desire should begin with the obvious — all the events that cause happiness. More subtly, however, we must recognize that sexual behavior can be motivated by the need to defend against loneliness, sadness, or anxiety. Of course, the processes that we discussed in the previous chapters — falling in love, being in love, the attainment of psychological intimacy — and whatever may lead to a renewed appreciation of the partner, are stimuli for desire. This renewed appreciation can also be created by the threat of loss of a sexual partner through accident or illness, or one of the couple's extramarital sexual experiences. The processes that lead to forgiveness (see Chapter 6) can stimulate a renewed sexual interest. When constructing a list of such stimuli, most people would include, at least for males, the varieties of pornography. These include magazines, Internet material, Internet chat opportunities, reading erotic portions of literature or love stories without explicit sexual descriptions. The anticipation of commercial sex or sex with a chat room partner stimulates desire. Women's desire to become pregnant is powerful. Those who can comfortably do so use their memories of previous sexually exciting experiences and conjuring of erotic fantasies to provoke arousal. When people strongly identify as sexual beings, they often use memory and fantasy to maintain a state of excitement for themselves. Some people are certain that low doses of substances of abuse work for them (Schiavi & Segraves, 1995). Finally, as therapists, we may have witnessed the increase in desire that follows an individual or a couple overcoming an impediment to pleasure through education, psychotherapy (see Chapter 8), or medical treatment of a sexual dysfunction.

Individuals and couples have to integrate some of these strategies in order to maintain a sexual life for decades while staying in love. One of the most vital stimuli on this list is the appreciation of the love one has for a partner. We have previously discussed the internalized image of the partner as beloved being the product of positive appraisals. Over a period of years these positive appraisals generate a habit of bestowals that create a strong motive to behave sexually.

In the early phase of a sexual relationship, the perception of the partner's desire for us stimulates our desire for the partner. We feel wanted and that makes us want the ensuing arousal. We are experiencing the accreditation ceremony (Bergner, 2005). The problem arises as the being-in-love phase moves into the challenges of the staying-in-love phase. When a partner inevitably becomes neutral to slightly negative on occasion, the other is deprived of the stimulus for personal desire. Clinicians need to remain mindful of the importance of the interactive aspects of a couple's sexual equilibrium (Levine, 2005). This interaction can either enable or stifle sexual pleasure. In Chapter 6, we will consider the phenomenon that occurs in some extramarital affairs when both people once again have their desire stimulated by the new partner's desire.

SEXUAL DESIRE PARADOXES

Sunny motivations for sex are easy to discuss in public: attachment, loving, reproduction, nurturing a partner, and having fun. It is far more difficult to talk about the paradoxes of desire that are just an ordinary part of the human erotic landscape.

1. *Sexual drive and motivation are not necessarily in sync.* When a person experiences sexual drive manifestations, these are not necessarily directed toward the socially acceptable partner. A person can be suffused with drive, for instance, but have no motivation to bring his or her body to the partner for sex. Clinicians often encounter patients who are too angry, fearful, disappointed, or alienated to make love to their partners. On the chart, they may score 2+ for drive but 0 for motivation. When they are given the diagnosis of acquired hypoactive sexual desire disorder, the clinician must grasp that the patient's mind refuses to allow its expression with the partner.

2. *Behavioral fidelity and mental infidelity.* The cultural ideals of love emphasize fidelity. This expectation is so strong that thoughts of sex with another person, let alone flirtations or nongenital physical intimacies, often provoke guilt and secrecy. Despite this expectation and

the widespread reinforcement of it by major cultural institutions, even the most earnest of individuals find it impossible to banish all unfaithful thoughts. For many, the idea of even attempting to eradicate them from consciousness is a useless, unsophisticated ambition. (Humor is a better solution.) One cannot live a long life, even when happily situated in marriage, without an occasional extramarital mental excursion.

3. *Lust.* Images of attractive young people engaging in consenting pleasant sexual behaviors are sexually exciting to watch. Images of attractive naked bodies displayed in an appealing fashion are similarly arousing. These images create efficient sexual arousal — particularly for the young. They reduce our sexuality to its simplest aesthetic form, unfettered by ordinary psychological, social, and moral complexity. They induce an intense desire for orgasm. This capacity for lust is hardwired into our brains. It exists in both genders regardless of the person's moral sensibilities against the stimulation.

4. *Sexual expression is less fettered with derogation.* Some men subjectively notice that they are more interested in sexual behaviors and less inhibited during them if they perceive the partner to be of lesser social quality than themselves. This is entirely a subjective judgment that rests upon the man's values. Her "inferiority" may involve education, ethnicity, beauty, economic status, intelligence, voca-

tion, power in an organizational hierarchy, and other matters. The oft-quoted madonna–whore concept that women are either the marrying kind or the sexual kind, refers to this male tendency. Some men cannot feel sexual interest if they know too much about the woman's person or value her as an equal or superior. The strains of this paradox — men's eroticism may not prefer social and political equality — can be seen at various stages in a man's life (Freud, 1912). It is encoded in the notion of a sultan owning a harem. This tendency is known to exist in women's eroticism, but I am uncertain about its prevalence or persistence.

5. *Familiarity diminishes sexual interest.* If we are successful in negotiating the dangerous waters of long-term monogamous unions, we set ourselves up for the problem of familiarity (Mitchell, 2002). Staying in love for a long time allows a couple to explore numerous avenues of sexual expression and grow into and out of various pleasures. After a certain time, however, the couple has done everything that they can comfortably and excitedly share. Sexual behavior may be experienced as duller as a result at least by one of them. Many faithful individuals can count on ~3000 sexual experiences with their life partner. Somewhere along the way, longing for the novelty of a new partner triggers the infidelity paradox.

Sexual Desire Disorders

The concept of a sexual desire disorder is only one generation old. Freud, for all his emphasis on instinctual libido and sexual development, defined only one desire disorder: Oedipal inhibition of sexual love for a spouse (Freud, 1905). Masters and Johnson identified no such connection (Masters & Johnson, 1970). Lief and Kaplan's (Kaplan, 1977) separate proposals (Kaplan, 1976) for a desire diagnosis were accepted in *DSM-III-R* in 1980 (American Psychiatric Association, 1980).

All efforts to elucidate a single pathogenesis of hypoactive sexual desire disorder and sexual aversion have failed. Today, these diagnoses are perceived to be a rich mixture of patterns involving biological, psychological, and cultural factors (Basson, 2006). Three more desire diagnoses might be useful for a future nosology. The first would capture the phenomenon of the dissipation of sexual desire as a consequence of another sexual dysfunction. For instance, a woman's inability to attain orgasm with her partner in her 20s predisposes her to lose sexual interest as she gets older. The second would separate those cases in which a man or a woman's life is plagued by the inability to experience sexual desire and love for the same person. The third pattern is a product of the Internet. Now we see many men who have become addicted to sexual stimulation using their computers. They might be said to have hyperactive sexual desire, sexual compulsivity, or addiction (Stein, Black, Shapira, & Spitzer,

2001), although many of them have lost sexual interest in their real partners. Then again, if desire is ever widely perceived as being only early arousal, perhaps a future nosology would only list arousal and orgasmic disorders just as Masters and Johnson proposed in 1970.

THE ASSESSMENT OF DESIRE DISORDERS

Ideally we assess sexual desire complaints by considering each of the three components of sexual desire. We ask ourselves if there is an old or new deficiency of sexual drive. If the answer is that the deficiency is relatively new, we consider the medical causes of diminished drive. If the answer is that the absence of drive has been present since the onset of partnered sexual life, we turn to individual and interpersonal factors to examine the motives for avoiding sexual behavior. We want to clearly identify and respond to them by bluntly articulating the patient's reasons for sexual avoidance. We then share our views about what needs to occur to regain willingness to make love and set about creating those conditions. If the problem seems to be resulting from a rigid or constricted notion of normality or never outgrown unsophisticated concepts of sexual morality, we turn our efforts toward supportive education to facilitate a less punitive approach to sexual expression (McCarthy & McCarthy, 2003).

Clinicians often divide women's loss of desire into pre- and postmenopausal categories. There is a great research effort to find medication for postmenopausal women because the loss of desire with menopause is thought to be biogenic (Dennerstein, 2003). Thus far clinicians only have the promise of a remedy. There are no FDA-approved medications for this problem, although many physicians are prescribing testosterone for this purpose (Davis, Davison, Donath, & Bell, 2005; North American Menopause Society, 2005).

The motivational component of sexual desire cannot be understood apart from the subjects of love and psychological intimacy. Patients bring up these subjects with their unclearly defined terms for love and intimacy (Brezsnyak & Whisman, 2004). In the therapies that I conduct, I use the specific concepts of love, psychological intimacy, and sexual desire that the reader has just encountered. These concepts assist patients in better understanding what has long been occurring in the privacy of their minds and relationships. I put into words what has been inchoate for them and this process generates hope and energy. When people arrive for therapy, they typically feel hopelessly trapped in their position on the desire spectrum. But stopping a medication, having an intimate discussion with their spouse, talking over some nonsexual issue with nonjudgmental frankness and clarity in therapy, can immediately shift their position on the spectrum to the right.

SEXUAL DESIRE IS OUR PRIVATE TEACHER

By paying attention to our desires from about age 10 on (Herdt & McClintock, 2000), we learn about our gender identity, orientation, and intention (Levine, 1997). Within several years, we classify ourselves, based on our pattern of desire, as sexually ordinary or as having some unconventional sexual identity status. Our sexual desires soon introduce us to the possibility of masturbation, which we have to come to grips with in terms of our values. Desire forces us to confront our aesthetic tastes as we realize how we feel and think about beauty in terms of age, race, and physical characteristics. We then may begin to reflect on our earliest sensibilities about any would-be partners' social assets such as their intelligence, talent, values, and economic and social potential. As new relationships evolve, our sexual desires help us to decide when, if ever, we will aspire to monogamy. They help us to proceed to exclusivity or not to go forward with another person. On a daily basis, in all intimate relationships, our sexual desires reflect how we still think and feel about what happened yesterday between us. By watching the ebb and flow of our desire, we come to suspect that there is some explanation for when we want to make love.

Sexual desire educates us throughout our lives. It often reflects our longing for something that we do not currently have. Since almost all lives are periodically unsatisfying, our new sexual desires inform us about our felt deficiencies in ourselves and our relationships and how they might be improved.

Behavioral Science and Sexual Desire

Both the clinical and the scientific approaches to desire have distinct important limitations. Although clinicians can richly conceptualize sexual desire (Schnarch, 2000) and know that its subjective and behavioral manifestations ebb and flow, we are not much help to scientists who need to measure it. We can speak of sexual fantasies, sexual dreams, masturbation, initiation of sexual behavior with a partner, receptivity to the partner's initiation of sex, genital sensations, or heightened responsivity to erotic cues in the environment and know that we are referring only to aspects of desire. However, we cannot suggest a sample of this list that would adequately capture sexual desire for research purposes. Currently, those who do research in this arena reduce the complexity of desire to an almost homogeneous force. They speak only of sexual desire, often as distinct from the motivation to have sex (Basson, 2006). They then scale the force on 1 to 5 or 1 to 7 scales. Here is an approach to measuring men's sexual desire that studies of the PDE-5 inhibitors (i.e., Viagra, Levitra and Cialis) employed (Rosen et al., 1997).

> Sexual desire is a feeling that may include wanting to have a sexual experience, for instance intercourse or masturbation, thinking about having sex, or feeling frustrated due to lack of sex.
> Over the past four weeks, have you felt sexual desire?
> Over the past four weeks, how would you rate your level of sexual desire?

This measurement failed to document an increase in sexual desire as a result of taking Viagra, Levitra, or Cialis, even though other measurements documented an increased frequency of sexual behavior. The measurement of women's sexual desire in drug trials is even more of a challenge. In several important trials, nine questions rated 1 to 5 or 1 to 7 are being used. The numbers are added up to define the level of a research subject's sexual desire (Simon et al., 2005). Data such as 36 before the drug, 49 after the drug are obtained. One cannot be certain, however, whether the subjects are feeling more drive, motivation, arousal, pleasure, or hope.

Sexual desire, which is the sum of the forces that incline us toward, or lean us away from sexual behavior, is a rich, vital, but elusive concept. Sexual desire is like a cloverleaf in a highway system. Many roads lead to it and many emerge from it. However tangible we wish desire to be, there is something metaphorical about it. One day, perhaps its neurophysiologic essence will be discovered.

6. Infidelity
Vital Background Concepts

Introduction

It seems only natural to have a chapter on infidelity in a book about love because my patients, faithful and unfaithful, have been discussing the two subjects in juxtaposition for years. There are, however, far more compelling reasons for clinicians to turn their careful attention to this topic. Infidelity further illuminates our quest for love and satisfying sex. It reminds us that the heralded ambitions of love are not attained by many people. It demonstrates the risks that people are willing to take and compromises they are willing to make, when they realize that because of themselves, their partner, or their fate, they are not on course to attain a sufficient portion of love's ideals. Infidelity helps us to define and understand that sacrifices are required for living up to those ideals. Finally, infidelity reminds us that some adults do believe that the ideals of love are illusions.

Motives Vary

Infidelity cannot be dismissed with any single explanation (Lusterman, 1998; Weil, 2003). While many of the unfaithful seem to be seeking love, others seem to be seeking pleasurable sex. They pursue experiences that keep their lives interesting, their sex exciting, and their sense of themselves as adventuresome. There are yet others whose extramarital sexual activities* seem to be motivated by the wish to distract themselves from painful aspects of their lives. And, some of this behavior seems to be related to acute or longstanding psychiatric illness.

We are often called upon to understand the motives for infidelity among our patients. This can be a significant challenge. Three obstacles may stand in our way. Some patients remain uncertain that it is safe to reveal their motives. Others are genuinely baffled by their patterns. Our personal moral and ideological biases may limit accurate perceptions as well as lead us to pejoratively interpret such behaviors. It is my hope that this and the following chapter will assist clinicians in finding a fresh approach to the subject.

Public Views

Infidelity is a violation of one of love's basic tenets. Its occurrences deeply disappoint us because we want to believe in love's

---

* I will use this term with the reader's understanding that it also applies to unmarried couples, including same-sex pairs.

potential to generate continuing happiness, mental health, and sexual pleasures. We often want to blame someone for the violation and ostracize the perpetrator ("pig!" "slut!"). When we inhabit this punishing mode, we are not interested in how it came about or the positive purposes that it served. Lurking behind such responses is an uncomfortable awareness of the tenuousness of many relationships. We don't want to acknowledge that we too may feel that we have not attained love's great goals or that at one time we may have seriously considered an extramarital option. It is easier to assert a monolithic moral opposition to infidelity. We want to teach our children that fidelity is required in order to have a good family life. We suspect any offering of a contrary idea to be psychobabble, rationalization, or moral depravity. In American public political arenas, almost everything that is ever said about it conveys social opprobrium. In the arts arena, however, comedy, fiction, movies, and the theater sometimes provide us with an opportunity to understand the subject in a more nuanced manner.

Countertransference

Most mental health professionals have had little to no consideration of infidelity in their training programs. The public view that surrounds us in the culture may have been our only view as we grew into our professional roles. When we begin to hear infidelity stories, our shock and emotional stirrings threaten our ability to remain nonjudgmental, calm, nondirective, and clear thinking.

When therapists have had no awareness of an episode of extramarital sex in their families of origin and have been faithful in their relationships, they will react to their first encounters with various situations of infidelity in expected ways. Here are four common situations:

- A patient is seriously considering his or her first extramarital sex;
- A patient has just recently become involved in extramarital sex;
- A patient is just ending such a relationship;
- A patient is intensely missing an ended extramarital relationship.

Our responses are likely to be an array of anxiety, anger, envy, sympathy, moral superiority, and disdain in varying combinations and intensities. When we listen to those who are distressed about their partner's newly discovered infidelity, the range of feelings may include awe, sympathy, and relief that it has not happened to us. When we work with a couple in these circumstances, we may feel differently about each partner for a while. We must be vigilant about behaving in an evenhanded manner.

We have more complex countertransference reactions when we have a personal relationship to infidelity. Our internal responses change if we are currently having an affair, if we have already had several affairs, if our spouse has been unfaithful, and if our parents' marriage was characterized by infidelity. These situations link our personal feelings about the patient to our personal lives in an even more riveting manner. Dealing with infidelity can be an emotionally exhausting burden.

Privacy and Secrecy

Privacy is the word that we use when we have agreed by social convention not to discuss a matter that we know exists. Urination, defecation, menstruation, and sexual behavior are enveloped in such privacy. Privacy is a form of a boundary.

> *9-year-old Sara, giggling:* Daddy, do you and Mommy have sex?
>
> *Calm father:* Yes.
>
> *A further emboldened Sara:* Daddy, did you and Mommy have sex last night?
>
> *Surprised father:* Sara, darling, that is none of your business!

Father is illustrating the concept of sexual privacy. Of course, Sara's parents have sex and she is entitled to know that. Sex is an ordinary, expected, desired part of marriage and Sara's father wants to speak positively about it. But there are limits about what parents will reveal about private matters. He supports Sara's right to know the truth as she is coming to learn about matters that she did not appreciate just a short time ago. But privacy contains a functional boundary. Even if he and his wife had sex last night, Sara does not have a right to that information. None of this is a secret.

A secret is something that a person prefers to remain unknown and that he or she will mislead others about to keep them from learning about its occurrence. The desire to appear innocent of an act instantly creates the prevarication. Extramarital sex is usually a secret from a partner. When first directly asked about it, particularly if the person questioned is unsure about what facts are at the confronter's disposal, most people, even "honest" ones, will initially deny the infidelity.

Infidelity can be a private matter or a secret. Many couples who have known infidelity in their relationship prefer to keep this a private matter between them. They do not want their friends, family, and children to know that it occurred. They have their reasons. Many unfaithful people, however, carefully guard their secret from everyone. They, too, have their reasons. Others share their infidelity as a private communication with a friend or friends who are expected to collude in maintaining their secret from the spouse.

Sexual secrets tend to become sexual privacies as people mature. Many young people have sexual impulses, temptations, longings, or behaviors that they don't want to think about or label. They keep secrets from themselves. Therapists commonly encounter men whose homoerotic longings were not acknowledged to themselves for many years. Couples' common secrets from one another include masturbation, extramarital flirtations/ temptations, and longings for a more exciting partner. These are better regarded as privacies. A married man's homosexual longings can remain a private matter if he and his wife understand that each of them has the right to and need for an erotic privacy boundary. To protect her from distress, he does not reveal to her his homoerotic desires and to protect him from distress, she does not tell him about her desires for other men. Secrecy about such matters is created when partners do not realize that marriage cannot prevent attractions to others for a lifetime. Masturbation, pornography, and erotic tension with someone outside the marriage can be regarded as private matters or secrets depending on the partners' sensibilities.

Guilt and Shame

Guilt is the expected accompaniment to extramarital sex. The unfaithful person is aware that he or she has betrayed the partner and has not lived up to a personal vow, even when the partner is unaware. This guilt is not only a thought process; it is also a state of unease. For many, the unease predominates during sleeping times. Over time guilt can be worked through significantly and lessened.

When the extramarital sex is discovered the betrayal changes character. The partner reacts, often with great pain, and the perpetrator's guilt intensifies. Shame is added to the guilt when the perpetrator faces the partner. If the betrayed person shares the news with family and friends, the perpetrator's guilt is complicated by his or her new negative social status in their eyes. Shame intensifies.

Guilt is not, however, the invariable accompaniment to extramarital sex. Those who feel entitled to sexual experiences outside their marriage do not experience guilt. But, they can still be shamed by their behavior.

Infidelity Is Dangerous!

Danger is inherent in infidelity. The immediate dangers are the changes in personal identity, guilt, and, of course, unwanted discovery. There are even greater longer term risks. These involve the ultimate restructuring of the marriage and family life. Discovered infidelity can reorder how we relate to each family member and to our circle of friends. It can immediately change our sexual opportunities at home and limit the quality of our sexual function with new partners. It rearranges our income as well as how we spend our time. Some unfaithful people are deliberately seeking a way to restructure their lives. Those who are not are often unhappily surprised by how little control they have over the changes in their lives. Nightmarish outcomes include an extramarital pregnancy, the appearance of a mental illness, or a suicide among the unfaithful, the spouse, or the other person. These same catastrophes can occur among older children as they react to the changes in the structure of their families. Statistical information about such risks is lacking, but clinicians have plenty of anecdotes.

Epidemiology

All mainstream cultural and religious institutions look askance at extramarital behavior. Up to 80% of the American and British populace consider it to be morally wrong (Barlow, Duncan, James, & Park, 2001; Thornton & Young-DeMarco, 2001). People gossip about infidelity, expressing disappointment and disapproval to friends. The fear of gossip may limit unfaithfulness by threatening the reputations of the indiscreet (Bergmann, 1993). Despite these forces of social control, at least 20% of married men and 10% of married women become involved sexually with someone other than a spouse. The rates for American women less than age 40 equal the male rate (Wiederman, 1997). Estimates of previous infidelity among the divorced exceed 50% (Kontula & Haavio-Mannila, 2004). Infidelity is not rare.

Sociologists and anthropologists have described the diverse forms of infidelity and have suggested various ways to understand it (Duncombe, Harrison, Allan, & Marsden, 2004). But these survey-based scientific approaches are limited by three methodological obstacles: the research subject's need for privacy; the lack of confidence in how to ascertain motives for the infidelity; lack of certainty about the appropriate measures of outcomes. Scientists are still uncertain about how gender, age, class, and ethnicity influence motivations for infidelity. They do not understand how culture modifies private psychological reactions to a spouse's infidelity (Morgan, 2004). For example, do women not get as upset in cultures where men are expected to be unfaithful at least occasionally (Scheinkman, 2005)? There are so many forms and degrees of infidelity that prevalence studies fail to capture the personal struggles about sexual fidelity and betrayal (Levine, 1998). Some argue that prevalence data grossly underestimate the human experience with infidelity (Kipnis, 2004).

The Therapist's Role

In dealing with the emotional turbulences associated with revelations of extramarital sex, clinicians should aspire to maintain personal balance and to think clearly. It is not our role to enforce the public rules of marriage or to recommend divorce. If we seem to be rigorously against infidelity, our patients will eventually question our objectivity and knowledge of subjective mental life. We are expected to understand that extramarital sexual behavior benefits men and women in ways that cannot be easily spoken about in public. We are also expected to know that some men and women highly value their extramarital experiences and do not experience major regret over time (Wright, 1994). We also need to recognize that many unfaithful males report that they know of no married peers who abstain from all forms of extramarital sex. On the other hand, if we seem to be rigorously in favor of infidelity, many people would not seek our services. Our quiet nonpolitical sophistication about the world of sexual possibilities, and their potential benefits and destructiveness, seem to serve us best in this affectively powerful arena.

A LICENSE TO BE CURIOUS

When alone with our patients, we assume that we are the most expert person present when it comes to mental health and mental disorders. This is often so, but in dealing with infidelity our attitude should not provide a hint of arrogance. We should reflect the idea that we are less the knowledgeable authority and more the curious student of the problem. In the face of an acutely aggrieved spouse, we should try not to formulate simple causal explanations such as, "Your husband is such a narcissist"; "Your wife is rebelling against your dictatorial style." Single hypotheses of individual or marital psychopathology are rarely a sufficient account of the actual circumstances, despite what our professional traditions may have taught us (Brown, 1999; Moultrup, 1990; Pittman, 1989; Strean, 1980). Such formulations, masquerading as erudition, often reveal our personal values, identification with an ideology, sympathy with the cuckold, gender biases, or failure to consider the power of sexual frustration.

A more complete explanation requires time and trust, and must include a grasp of the conscious decision-making processes of the unfaithful person. The unfaithful justify their involvement to themselves. We should be interested in their thinking (Weeks, Gambescia, & Jenkins, 2003). We have a license to be curious and a responsibility to provide explanations that reflect the answers to our many inquiries. Does the patient's thinking primarily focus on sexual or nonsexual interpersonal frustration?

Is it more about the partner or the patient? Does it seem rational or irrational to the patient? What influence have peers had on the decision? How important is alcohol or substance abuse to its occurrence? Did parents or siblings have affairs? Did the person enter into the new arrangement with the intention of maintaining the social, economic, and child-rearing functions of the marriage for the foreseeable future? Did the person enter into the infidelity feeling close to the personal decision to divorce? If so, did it solidify the decision, lead to a reinvestment in the marriage, or have little impact? Did the person enter into the infidelity having already decided to divorce? Did they consider what they did to be infidelity? What makes giving up the current extramarital relationship difficult? These questions reflect our assumption that motives can derive from family of origin forces, marital relationship forces, and from forces within the affair. The questions provide an antidote for simplistic thinking.

Our discussions with the patient about motives should be fair, comprehensive, and without moral disapproval. In order to attain this goal, we might ask ourselves to conceptualize the options any committed responsible adult has when he or she becomes consistently and deeply disappointed with a partner's attitudes, behaviors, and sexual responses. When sex is consistently nowhere close to frequent, pleasurable, or exciting, when the partner does not enjoy it, cannot relax, cannot attain orgasm, and cannot discuss the situation, what do we think should be done? Visit a primary care physician? Take a medication? Seek sex or marital therapy, devalue previous expectations, find a new important recreation, or rely on masturbation?

The Lexicon of Infidelity

Most of the commonly employed synonyms for infidelity connote moral disapproval, bad character, or sickness. They indicate that infidelity occurs over a wide range of circumstances. Some common verbs are *cheating, betraying, deceiving; sexual adventuring, swinging, partner swapping*. Here are some nouns: *philanderer, womanizer, slut, tart, whore; affair, affair of the heart, love affair; adultery, dalliance, indiscretion, just-sex, fling, one-night stand, casual sex, sex buddy*. The broader terms *sexual addict* and *acting out* often include infidelity.

ACTING OUT

We professionals often refer to infidelity as acting out. This term has at least six meanings, which I can sometimes discern from context clues. It can mean that the behaviors: (1) are disapproved of in a conventional sense; (2) express a fantasy; (3) risk negative consequences; (4) are created by individual psychopathology; (5) are motivated by unconscious forces; (6) occur because the person does not have the capacity to put into words what he or she is actually experiencing.

What is and what is not infidelity? When this question has to be asked in a clinical situation, rather than authoritatively answering it, the therapist is usually wiser to rely on the patients' sensibilities. When a patient's sensibility seems too severe, we may raise a question about whether infidelity is being employed as a simile to convey that "I feel *as if* you were unfaithful to me when you…." Concepts of what is acceptable and what is not acceptable vary (Bergner & Bridges, 2002). For some wives, for example, the husband's viewing of pornography is an act of infidelity while for others it is "boys will be boys." Disagreement can exist within a couple about whether a behavior constituted an act of infidelity. This should not be surprising since there is disagreement among people about what even constitutes sex (Faulkner, 2003; Randall & Byers, 2003). Some writers consider infidelity to be anything that occurs between a married person and someone other than a spouse that decreases the intimacy and increases the emotional distance between the spouses (Moultrup, 1990). Such broad definitions remind us that sexual infidelity is only one way in which a man or woman can emotionally leave a partner.

I prefer to remind myself that infidelity is also an opportunity and that a calm therapist is part of that chance to transform crisis into something positive (Frank, 2005).

> By tracking down a $500 charge for a gift to a stranger, a wife discovered that her overworking, sexually disinterested husband of 25 years had in the past year become a frequenter of strip clubs — the gift was for one of the strippers. Distressed, she returned to her psychiatrist who recommended that she divorce her always weird, now sexually addicted, husband. The woman, however, was curious about what her husband was experiencing — it was so out of character — and insisted

that he take her there. She was amazed. Boldly, she arranged to meet the gift recipient for coffee and learned not only about her husband, but learned also about the culture of the club and what the dancers did. Such conversations and regular attendance with her husband on weekends enabled her to overcome her lifelong prudishness. From her underwear to her outerwear, she changed how she dressed. She became orgasmic again after marriage-long anorgasmia. Their sexual frequency went from three to four times per year to that many times per week. The couple went to strip clubs regularly together for about six months before attendance became occasional. Their sexual life, however, remained far better than it had been throughout their marriage.

The Internet has provided many new opportunities for infidelity. Couples have to decide whether viewing naked women for hours most nights at home fractures a marital vow. They have to confront the meaning of the activity's secrecy. Other activities, such as chatting anonymously with strangers about sex, exchanging pictures of personal sexual anatomy, or meeting the person for sexual activity usually throw spouses into the profound emotional storms of infidelity crises.

Affairs Begin with Flirting

Flirtation is early courtship behavior, a means of getting the erotic attention of another. Its observable mechanisms involve prolonged eye contact, apparent interest or enjoyment in the person's conversation, standing or sitting close to the person, and a slight excess of innocuous touching (Ackerman, 1994). No verbal expressions of personal interest are necessary to create the excitement that comes from the realization that this other person is interested.

For the flirting person, the behavior creates a tantalizing, promising, exciting *un*certainty (Philips, 1994). The motivation to create such uncertainty is not necessarily to initiate an affair. It can be to make social occasions less boring; to affirm one's attractiveness, social worth, or power to provoke the interest of others; to pretend to oneself that one has more relationship possibilities than one knows that one has; to celebrate the overcoming of one's former social shyness and sense of social inadequacy; to provoke sexual desire in oneself or another person; or to present a false impression to others of oneself as a comfortable sexual person. Some consider their flirtation to be a harmless social game without the risk of sexual behavior because they withdraw when the other person is responsive.

Flirtation changes its character when its signal is received with serious interest. Intimate talk, arranging for the next intimate conversation, and escalation of intrapsychic arousal and erotic imagery then quickly occur. Soon both individuals know exactly what is transpiring.

Some adults decide that well-chosen extramarital liaisons are part of their pleasure in living. They become skillful at negotiating for them. They privately reject the rule of fidelity. They are looking for sex, friendship, and a relationship without the mundane obligations of domestic life. "I have no interest in doing his laundry"; "I am not looking for love"; "This is fun."

The newly clandestine couple can be surprised, of course, by the sensations of love that arise as a result of their circumscribed meetings together. They can be taken aback by their yearning to establish a fuller life together. When both come to feel this way, a new set of problems unfurl. When yearnings are one-sided, a separate set of problems appear.

Infidelity and Values

It is likely to be shocking to many clinicians that every adult does not believe that fidelity is a necessity, a good thing, or even possible to attain. Most of those who hold such beliefs are unwilling to make their views widely known. I was taken aback the first time patients told me such things. I assumed that they were about to tell me of their membership in a Bondage/Domination Society or a Swingers' Club. I was wrong.

Beverly, a highly religious, extremely bright and accomplished grandmother and high-level administrator, is long married to a highly capable man she has continuously loved since college. After 35 years together they emanate warmth, respect, and mutual affection. Beverly, a high sex-drive person, discovered before marriage that her fiancé was nervous sexually and could rarely ejaculate. He improved somewhat over time and even more so in response to therapy, but he continues to have less sexual drive, to be less comfortable, and to not be able to be sensuous enough to regularly attain orgasm. When we met 20 years ago, they had long since worked out an arrangement that enabled her to have a sequence of friend-lovers. Her husband knows some of them personally, but prefers not to interact with them. Beverly keeps him informed about their identities and when she is with them. I was skeptical that this arrangement was acceptable to him, but having seen them periodically for two decades, I continue to believe his statements. "Beverly is a very sexual woman. I satisfy her in every other way, but not sexually. We love each other very much." Beverly periodically sees me when she is depressed over her job or when she is between friend-lovers. Her husband, who comes from a family with several depressive and obsessive-compulsive primary relatives, is seen annually to renew an SSRI, which has helped his dysthymia. Beverly's happiness about being able to make love by far outweighs his discomfort that she is with another man. He says, "Beverly is a wonderful person."

Beverly and her husband pay a price for how they live. The husband is not jolly during her times out and Beverly, who gets attached to her lovers, suffers grief and loneliness when these relationships end. Their price is balanced in their minds by the price of fidelity for them.

These days, I consider what people say about fidelity and infidelity as value statements. I discern three general values positions on infidelity. The conventional one strongly endorses fidelity as a basic requirement for love. This belief organizes and regulates social and sexual behavior until death of the partner or the legal termination of the marriage. The position holds that the morality of fidelity is never relative or flexible. It is the rule, period — forever!

> Samuel, one of the first older patients I worked with who had psycho-genic impotence, believed this. After three years of devoted care of his wife in their home, she further deteriorated over the next two years in an Alzheimer's ward. She no longer could recognize him. After much prodding by his adult children who were trying to help him over his depression, he found "an angel," but could not have intercourse. Although he claimed to want to have intercourse, his penis seemed to have different ideas. After three emotional talks with me, he had inter-course successfully. But the next day, he was rushed to the hospital

with chest pain. A day later he was discharged with no cardiac diagnosis. For Samuel, angel or no angel, fidelity meant as long as she lives.

Robert, a 51-year-old minister being considered for bariatric surgery, proudly spoke of his fidelity during the last 12 years. A dozen years ago, his then 37-year-old wife, who never seemed to like sex or to have found it important for herself, announced that she wanted no further part of it after her second child was born. Robert felt caught between his religious concept of having married for better or for worse and his wish to have sex. After a few sulky arguments, he decided "not to push the issue for a while." He returned to masturbation. It was during these dozen years that he lost control of his eating. His wife has repeatedly expressed worry about his weight but sex is not discussed.

The second position rejects fidelity as a fundamental requirement for love. It also powerfully organizes and regulates social and sexual behavior. It is well hidden because to discuss it is to risk widespread social censure. The second position holds that this moral matter needs to be understood in a nuanced and flexible manner. Fidelity is perhaps ideal but in the reality of people's lives the inability to realize the ideal does not mean that love does not exist. Beverly and her husband wish to be together until death. They began with traditional fidelity values but their positions changed as they were deciding to marry. Most others who switch from the first to the second value positions reach that decision later in the marriage.

The shift in values concerning fidelity does not seem quite as surprising when we realize that other values change. Remaining faithful for a lifetime to religious, political, or professional values proves to be quite difficult. Over a lifetime, many change their religious beliefs, affiliations, and practices. Others change their political views, parties, and activities. Clinicians change their therapy beliefs. This evolution of values is an ordinary outcome of maturation. As we move from an understanding of ethical and moral issues in black and white absolutist terms to comprehending the gray ambiguity of most matters, why should we expect that sexual values would not evolve? Views about fidelity do change in either direction as men and women accumulate life experience and new perspectives.

- After causing years of heartbreak, turmoil, and tension, a repeatedly unfaithful 50-year-old man stopped drinking and became convinced that fidelity was the only path for him. He started a movement in his church to encourage fidelity.
- After two decades of devotion to a husband who consistently failed to have a grasp of her emotional and sexual needs, a mother of two decided that she was foolish to not have some fun when an opportunity arose.

When values against infidelity are strong and effective, the dangers of flirtation, exposures to various extramarital temptations, and the possibility of outside sexual liaisons are minimized through discipline. These values work best when one is satisfied with one's love and sexual life.

Losing certainty about our values is not an easy process. As we move toward giving them up, we confront our ambivalence.

Our lives feel contradictory. We begin to feel alienated from those who strongly hold our previous values. When our values begin to evolve, we — ourselves and others — may think that we are rationalizing, that is, talking ourselves into a disengagement from our own moral principles. These descriptions apply to the loss of any values — religious, political, or sexual.

The disengagement from one's previous sexual values often occurs when a person has long been disappointed with the character and the incompatibility of the partner. Feeling hopelessly trapped in a relationship stimulates some people to rethink their lives even before they meet another person. Their values change in response to the sense of unfairness or their poor luck in marital life.

The third position stridently rejects fidelity as stifling to pleasure, against biological tendencies, an invitation to boredom, and the source of numerous woes. When couples share this position, they have sex outside their primary relationship (O'Neill & O'Neill, 1972). This position tends to be friendly to sexual minorities (Weitzman, 1999; Wright, 1994). Men tend to hold this view longer than do their female partners. But most of the time that this view exists, it is not shared with the partner. While clearly explained without ambivalence to oneself, the holder of this position has surreptitious extramarital sex. In some cultures in some eras, this idea has been incorporated as a divine right of males (Krakauer, 2003). The fact that kings were rarely expected to be faithful to their queens reminds people that this value system works to serve men's sexual desires over the life cycle far more than those of women.

Clinically we encounter people in the third position largely because the spouse is distressed or worried about the mental health underlying the partner's new behavioral patterns and statements. While we suspect hypomania, if the patient will spend some time with us, the person may be able to convince us that he or she no longer holds the same values. These patients educate us. The trouble is that many people who feel this way hide behind the first or second position, making it difficult for us to accurately perceive their motivations. All three value positions on fidelity can be found among both heterosexual and gay and lesbian couples.

Values Generate Meanings

An important relationship exists between values, meanings, and feelings. Our values, which are largely hidden from view, shape the meanings of events to us. Values evolve as we mature. This translates into the fact that a similar event has different meanings to us over time. Here are two examples:

(1) When beginning to masturbate some adolescents think they are sinning. Masturbation leads to anxiety, fear of negative consequences, guilt, and a fight to suppress the

behavior. A few years later, when they have learned it is a normal and moral behavior, self-stimulation will no longer generate negative feelings.

(2) An adolescent pregnancy may generate a suicidal crisis in a 16-year-old. Ten years later the same woman is apt to think differently about an unplanned pregnancy.

We are far more aware of our feelings than their meanings or the values they represent. It is not widely understood that feelings are the leading edge of the private meanings of an event and these, in turn, reflect our hidden values. A person's infidelity induces feelings in us instantly. As we think about our feelings we determine the meaning of the infidelity to us. From this meaning we can deduce our values about infidelity.

Who Are the Relevant Meaning Makers in Extramarital Sex?

All people are meaning makers — that is, they attribute personal meanings to events. When clinicians are called upon regarding the discovery of extramarital sex (we are not routinely), we can see that everyone involved has his or her own reactions to the behavior (Weeks et al., 2003). In the recently exposed clandestine love affair, the usual cast of meaning makers include the aggrieved partner, the person having the affair, the person with whom the affair is conducted, the older children, the confidant, parents, siblings, friends, and the mental health professional. Each finds and is entitled to separate meanings in the affair (Scheinkman, 2005). Each therefore experiences a different array of feelings about the affair.

7. Infidelity
The Work of the Therapist

Newly Discovered Infidelity

From what we typically get to see as clinicians, the discovery of a partner's infidelity quickly creates an emotional storm. The conceptual themes of the storm are difficult for the patient to detect and articulate because waves of sadness, anger, anxiety, shame, and vengeance pass through consciousness at a dizzying pace. Thoughts dart between the present, past, and future. The first ideas that are expressed by a betrayed person are related to the shock that "my partner would do such a thing" and "I can't believe that it happened to me." Four themes then reliably appear, but not with the simple clarity outlined here:

1. What is the personal meaning of the infidelity to me?
2. What is the best way I can respond to it?
3. Will I be abandoned?
4. Why did this happen?

The revelation of infidelity usually creates at least a two-person crisis. Both spouses feel rearranged by it. Each becomes anxious about undesirable restructuring of family relationships. Each may have separation anxiety, panic about being alone, generalized anxiety, or a return of old separation incapacities mixed into the emotional swirl.

The unfaithful person's identity as an honest person is changed; added to it is the burden of having caused this pain in the partner. The intensity of the betrayed partner's pain is often surprising to the spouse. Everything that they transact together for a while feels tense. Their children, even those who know nothing about the infidelity, react to the changes in the demeanor of their parents. The revelation ultimately humbles both spouses because it demonstrates that neither is in control of their destinies. While extramarital sex can unleash a firestorm of judgment against the unfaithful person, the betrayed partner also feels an intense mixture of loss and shame. Affairs convey, however erroneously, personal failure, as if the betrayed one caused the partner to decide and implement the new relationship.

As mental health professionals, we can help both spouses because we have a good sense of what is swirling within each of them. We calmly provide words for their concerns and feelings, offer an occasional reassurance, and suggest an agenda for what can be dealt with next (Gordon, Baucom, & Synder, 2004).

The Search for Motives

Both spouses eventually become interested in the motives for extramarital sex. Each may have a different tolerance for the layers of explanation. In an individual session when I first ask most patients why they were unfaithful, the answers are usually couched in uncertainty. Some then provide an account of separate converging considerations that led to the decision to be unfaithful. But when patients remain stymied, I try to overcome their obfuscation by using two history taking probes.

The first probe is directed at the patient's private value system. I ask the individual if the infidelity was a product of a closely held belief that "extramarital sex is fine for me as long my partner remains unaware." In using this question, I am exploring the patient's view of infidelity as a right, a privilege, or an entitlement. Positive answers reflect a current belief that the infidelity, in the grand scheme of things, is not a big deal.

> Yes, I had an affair because my husband was impaired by his preoccupation with his chronic illness. He had become so distant from my needs and me. That was the background for my new relationship. But, really I was out of town a lot, my supervisor had been helpful to me in my career, and it seemed like a harmless fun thing to do. And you know, it was a lot of fun, the sex was great, and we came to look forward to the next time we would be in the same out-of-town city. I don't regret our being together, what bothers me is how much I miss it.

The second probe explores whether the infidelity represents a rebellion against what exists with the spouse in the sphere of love or sex. Is the behavior a refusal to no longer passively endure a formidable obstacle to a higher quality of love?

> My wife does not really like sex. She does not get excited. She has not had an orgasm since we dated. We have become like brother and sister. I don't know if I can tolerate a life like this for much longer. I'm only 49. By God, I deserve some sexual pleasure.

> I concluded early in our marriage that my sweet cultured husband was gay but probably did not want me to know it. I doubt that he told himself because I was never aware that he had any sexual interests in anyone. We had our two children in the first three years of marriage and with few exceptions, never had sex again. I ran my business, we had an active community life, and I found four partners over a 25-year period. It is not as good as a normal sexual life, but I was not dealt those cards. I guess I should say to you that those were not the cards I dealt myself by choosing him. But I was young when I did that. In those days I thought all gay men were effeminate.

> After years of obedient celibacy, I decided that I don't believe the same things that I did during the early decades after ordination. I spent a lot of vacation time at my friends' house out of town. The three of us were together in the evenings but the wife and I spent all day together. We talked a great deal. She was receptive to my advances — or I was receptive to hers, who can tell? We had a lovely time. We did not have intercourse per se, but it was lovely. I thought about this a lot and concluded "nobody's perfect." Eventually, she felt she should stop and we did. I was sad.

After listening to the patient's discussion of these two large topics, I may summarize my own understanding of why he or she chose to have extramarital sex. I provide my hunches in an attempt to have patients explain themselves more honestly to themselves.

I don't assume that people are acting out on unconscious factors and that they therefore are unable to explain their motivations.

Motives vary considerably depending on when the infidelity occurs in the life cycle. At the beginning of relationships, prior to or during engagement, particularly when geographically separated from the partner, additional sexual experiences may occur. There may be uncertainty about going forward with the relationship, the wish to have a last hurrah, or the need to ascertain one's readiness for commitment. The unfaithful may use their sense of guilt and sexual pleasure to determine whether to proceed with their engagement. When partners learn about these involvements, they need to decide if such activities reflect a lack of belief in the personal need for fidelity and therefore predict a high risk of future infidelity.

During the last third of life, people recognize their time may be limited by illness or death. When opportunities arise that seem to hold something life changing or exciting for them, they may surprise themselves.

> Marjorie, a long married woman, asexual with her husband for several years, began a sexual relationship at age 69 with a 10-year younger woman, whose frank interest and self-revelations about lesbian experiences enticed her into a gradual sexual process that left her feeling exhilarated. Marjorie, who never sensed herself as either bisexual or hostile to lesbians felt no need to divorce. She had a great deal of respect and love for her husband, and felt no need to keep her lover from her house. Her husband was happy with his wife's new happiness over her friend but apparently did not suspect their sexual relationship.

He did ask once, however, if she thought her new friend was a bit of a lesbian and then joked that she better watch out.

Arnold, aged 67, could not obtain an erection two years after surgery for prostate cancer, despite his use of each of the three prosexual erectogenic drugs. He claimed to have never been unfaithful before. When at a convention out of town, he hired a young, beautiful prostitute to see if his problem had anything to do with his wife of 40 years whose memory was failing at a great rate. When he had no tumescence with the nice young woman, he concluded that his sexual life was over.

In summary, the search for motives is about the patient's own sense of entitlement to this behavior. As I listen, I try to discern whether the behavior is the result of:

- Longstanding personal values;
- Frustration in not being able to bring about a full enough two-way love relationship;
- A longstanding sense of masculine or feminine inadequacy;
- An attempt to see if a sexual dysfunction is partner-specific;
- A distraction from a more significant set of problems in the patient's life;
- A decision-making process about whether or not to permanently leave the relationship;
- The influence of peers;
- A fundamentally disordered mental state due to a psychiatric illness.

Seven Couple Therapy Obstacles and Suggestions for Overcoming Them

After the initial storm of discovered infidelity quiets down, we can continue to provide help to some individuals and couples. People can put extramarital sex behind them, but there are numerous obstacles to overcome before they can reestablish a kind, optimistic, psychological intimacy. These obstacles are an argument for having therapeutic assistance because each requires some reasonably authoritative guideline for the patient. The therapist in these situations is like a river guide taking people through waters with dangerous rapids. Sometimes they can paddle by themselves and sometimes they need to be told to shift their weight and paddle on the left side.

OBSTACLE 1. WHOSE INTERPRETATIONS OF THE AFFAIR ARE CORRECT?

We repeatedly hear passionate sentences such as, "I can't understand how you could do that!" or "Yes, we had a fling but it was nothing really." These sentences require further elaboration, but the elaborations cannot be provided because the distressed spouse is unable to pay attention. I authoritatively explain that the meanings of events are ultimately private and individual, and one person's meanings cannot be superimposed on the other.

John: Your affair was despicable; you are a moral degenerate who is not worthy of being in our children's presence!

Judy: You should at least consider what was happening before….

John: I'm not going to listen to any more of your bullshit rationalizations for your sinfulness.

Dr. Levine: John, today the meaning of Judy's affair to you is quite clear. Meanings have a way of evolving over time. I don't want us to lose sight of the fact that I am here trying to help each of you to work through your separate meanings of the affair. Then, one day *in the future* each of you can make decisions about how you want to relate to one another.

OBSTACLE 2. THE AGGRIEVED PARTNER INSISTS UPON KNOWING THE SEXUAL DETAILS OF THE INFIDELITY

The man, now trying to be honest, hesitates because he thinks the answers will only serve to hurt his wife further. I articulate each of their ambivalent positions. The wife may then decide whether to defer, obtain the details, or lose interest in the question. When a husband asks for such details of his wife's affair, her hesitation is more intense. Domestic violence often arises under such conditions (Whitehurst, 1971). I often say. "Can we wait to answer this question at another session because I'm not sure what is the best course? We all have to be wise about this. Such details after several days can be profoundly upsetting and provoke violence."

OBSTACLE 3. AN UNFAITHFUL PERSON ABRUPTLY ENDS AN AFFAIR FOR THE SAKE OF THE MARRIAGE AND IS PRIVATELY GRIEVING

The spouse is not likely to have any capacity to remain sympathetic as her or his partner silently recalls the sweet experiences of the past and feels sad. Rather, each time the preoccupation and sad demeanor of the partner are perceived, the spouse may be enraged and feel abandonment anxiety anew. My approach is to put equal weight on the grief and the inability to be calm in the face of it. I emphasize that the grief cannot and should not be denied.

OBSTACLE 4. THE ADVICE OF OTHERS TO SEPARATE OR DIVORCE IS QUOTED

In clarifying that I will not tell a person what to do about the marriage, I acknowledge that infidelity is a frequent reason for ending a marriage (Betzig, 1989) and add that if either partner has long been deeply unhappy with the unacceptable permanent limitations of the spouse as a life partner, he or she has a publicly justifiable reason to divorce. But if the spouse was not previously perceived as an unremitting heavy burden, each of them must decide in time, but not now, what to do about the marriage. I add that it is easy for others to say, "If that were my husband, I'd put him on the street." But, in my experience, pontificators often do not follow their own advice.

OBSTACLE 5. THE UNFAITHFUL PERSON ASKS FOR
FORGIVENESS AND AN END TO THE DISCUSSIONS

Getting beyond the emotional storm of a discovered affair usually takes longer than the impatient person hopes or expects. The pain seems to attenuate over time, but even if the experience is no longer mentioned, it is not forgotten — until dementia overtakes the spouse. Some people apologize, seek their partner's forgiveness, and search for spiritual rejuvenation. While research has not been able to clarify what predicts forgiveness (Fitcham, Paleari, & Regalia, 2002), forgiveness is a familiar religious topic (Puchalski, 2002; Wolpe, 2000). People on either side of an affair frequently reach out to their clergy. I deal indirectly with the impatience about being forgiven by giving my understanding of its three requirements. I announce that as far as I can tell, to be forgiven by anyone, the wrongdoer has to meet three conditions and demonstrate (1) personal clarity about wrongfulness of the behavior; (2) accurate knowledge of the specific consequences for the partner; and (3) persistent pervasive remorse. This trilogy has proven to be dramatically effective in diminishing the penitent's anger for not being forgiven.

Eventually, the betrayed partner realizes that he or she also longs to be done with the matter as well. The fruits of forgiveness for the aggrieved person include the dissipation of anger, ceasing to picture the actual sexual violations, ending of ruminations about what other options might have been undertaken, resignation to the possibility of recurrence; and surrendering the sense of moral superiority. The person knows that his or her continuing righteous indignation is an insufferable punishment and longs to lose it so as to feel generous and loving again.

Forgiveness does not mean that the bad behavior has been excused (Weeks, Gambescia, & Jenkins, 2003). The aggrieved will still think that the infidelity should not have happened. The aggrieved moral values may not change, although other aspects of the person invariably will.

Discussions about infidelity do end when the issues are thoroughly explored and respected. These discussions are typically exhausting for both partners. When they are over, the relationship does not return to where it had been; it begins from a different plateau.

OBSTACLE 6. THE RESUMPTION OF MUTUALLY DESIRED SEXUAL ACTIVITY

Some good clinical outcomes occur when spouses who previously thought they were entitled to extramarital sex are astounded at the pain they have caused and are appreciative of the partner's public grace during the turmoil — particularly the decision not to reveal the infidelity to friends and family. The couple can use sex to bond together anew because the unfaithful person feels such gratitude and freshly understands his or her fundamental need for fidelity. At the same time, the betrayed partner has clarified his or her wish to be married and to build upon their new psychological intimacy from weathering their crisis.

Many couples fail to reestablish a pleasurable sexual life together, however. The meanings of the event continue to remain powerfully affective. "He has been so good to me lately. Part of me wants to make love with him again, but a stronger part still says to punish him by refusing. I keep thinking of the dignity of not allowing it to return to normal. This is his third time in 45 years!" One episode of infidelity is a lot easier to overcome. Multiple episodes do not necessarily end the marriage, but they tend to end the couple's sexual life together.

The dignity of a wife can also be sorely assaulted by her husband's preoccupation with Internet pornography (Bergner & Bridges, 2002). Despite his protest that he has not been unfaithful, sex together may cease because she interprets his excitement to orgasm over other women's bodies as infidelity. Sometimes the man has confessed to his use of Internet pornography but not to the liaisons that emerged from his chat room adventures. In such cases, the woman is more accurate in her characterization than she knows.

Sometimes sex does not resume after the discovery of extramarital activity because the aggrieved person has a secret he or she cannot reveal: "I too have had an affair." This infidelity may have preceded or been reactive to the partner's recent affair. The aggrieved spouse, who is profoundly upset by the partner's betrayal, is trapped in a dilemma. The possibility of sex just makes the person relive the dilemma.

I laughed heartily when an enraged spouse told me about how she found revenge for her husband's recent affair by mixing her urine into his coffee one morning. Two months later, I was profoundly shocked to learn from her lover of 20 years that she had been sleeping with him periodically since high school. In the brief time I knew her, she refused to resume sex with her husband, relent in her criticism of his infidelity, reveal her infidelity, or continue talking to me. She was, I presume, trapped.

OBSTACLE 7. THE THREAT OF DIVORCE

In the rancor that may erupt after awareness of an affair, both partners may directly or indirectly threaten divorce. This creates separation anxiety and fears of abandonment in each partner, which can make useful discussions impossible. I try to explain that affairs are often the prelude to divorce because:

- The values of the partner have been so deeply offended that the aggrieved partner no longer feels as though the spouse has any redeeming value — that is, the extra-marital sex has extinguished all pleasure and interest in the partner as a person.

- The affair was undertaken because of private, profound unhappiness in the union that the unfaithful person could not effectively deal with. During the affair, the person unilaterally decided that the relationship was not fixable and decided to leave.

- The affair generated feelings, attitudes, and concerns that have proven beyond both partners' capacities to

work through and master. This reason provides motivation for hiring a therapist. All three people in the room
know, however, that even with our help one of them may
still decide to divorce.

Divorce puts all parties on a new developmental trajectory,
filled with uncertainties that cause almost everyone, however
inherently sound their mental health may be, considerable anxiety,
guilt, and regret. I emphasize to each member of the couple the
importance of separating the effects of affairs from the effects of
the decision to divorce. I advocate to them that they should make
no decision about what to do with the marriage, until the meanings and feelings about the affair can be articulated, understood,
and allowed to evolve. In the process someone brings up the experience of others who have restructured their lives in the hopes of
finding an improved social, sexual, emotional, and interpersonal
life. Some apparently accomplish their goals; others clearly have
not. Divorce rates of second marriages are sobering — 60 to 70%.
The ex-spouse or children who do not fare well are particularly
heavy burdens to consider in advance of the decision (Levine,
1999). The decision requires wisdom from both spouses.

The therapist provides patience and the recognition that some
marriages improve as a result of infidelity. Thoughtful discussions
provide both spouses with dignity because ultimately we all know
that temptations to infidelity are part of the human battle to maintain happiness, emotional intimacy, and mutually pleasurable sex.

Is Infidelity a Symptom of a Psychiatric Disorder?

"Is infidelity sick, doctor?" is one of the many questions that an aggrieved partner may ask the therapist. The undercurrent of such a question often is, "Will you join me in morally condemning my partner?" We generally do not.

But "Is infidelity a symptom of a psychiatric disorder?" is a reasonable question. It asks if a preexisting psychiatric disorder played a direct role in lowering moral restraints against infidelity or was its proximate cause. Sometimes the answer is "yes."

Joy, a faithful, tensely married, gregarious 31-year-old mother of two, worked as a pharmaceutical rep. She had regretted her marriage for at least three years and occasionally had fantasies of running away with a kinder man. Joy developed a mania about a week after her gynecologist put her on an SSRI. Before being hospitalized because of grandiosity, rapid speech, boundless energy, intolerance of sleep, and irritability, she had physical intimacies with three men within a 10-day period. When she stopped her medication and readily recovered from her mania, she was horrified over her behaviors and was paralyzed by her husband's cold, hostile label of *slut*. She resigned her job, lost her self-respect, and doubted even her minor decision making. She was far more depressed after her mania than when she began taking the SSRI.

I thought that her infidelity was largely a product of a toxic brain.

Rocco, a 50-year-old chronic alcoholic and sexual exhibitionist, who runs a successful home repair business, has been unfaithful to his wife of 26 years in a variety of ways, dating from their engagement period. As a teenager, he was frequently involved in fighting, truancy, and theft. He discovered leadership skills in the service. "I'm uneducated but street smart." His wife works full time. According to him, she is not aware of his recurrent exhibitionism to junior high school age girls or his many one night stands with women he is set up with by friends he meets in bars. His wife's parents care for their grandchildren by day and Rocco has supported his in-laws for over a decade. His wife joked with him for years about his girl friends during long periods of his sexual disinterest. Two years ago, without fanfare, after yet another episode of his binge drinking, she divorced him. She allowed him to remain in the house, however. Within two months, he returned to her bed. Three years later, they have forgotten about the divorce and are living as husband and wife. She has not learned of his two arrests for exhibitionism during one of which he was on relative house arrest with an ankle bracelet. Rocco told his family that he was being punished for driving while under the influence of alcohol. Rocco, who has never been violent or abusive in the home, is vital to everyone's financial health. His income is essential to the children's educational opportunities.

Rocco's numerous infidelities were a relatively minor part of his self-plaguing life patterns.

Frank is a college dropout who is periodically addicted to cocaine and pain medications. This twice divorced, devoted 52-year-old father, finally a success in his family's business, has not been able to stay interested in any woman. He is only attracted to those who are beautiful and young, but within several months of having conventional sex, he loses interest and develops erectile problems. His experiences with prostitutes allow him to feel normal. The pattern has repeated itself over 35 years.

Frank has a basic problem with integrating love and sex in his life. Fidelity would end all partner sexual behavior.

Linda is now normal weight as a result of gastric bypass surgery eight years ago. Her psychiatrist referred her for psychotherapy when she learned that Linda was contemplating having an affair. Linda explained to me that she was angry at her husband because of his lack of sympathy over her troubling weakness and fatigue from anemia. His impatience over her month of moping gathered up many of her other resentments — having to leave her friends when he took a job in this city; living in a house she didn't like; having to do everything while he is on his frequent business travels; his demands for sex when he returns; and the continuing anxiety that he will be transferred to another city uprooting her and their three children. Linda was not only avoiding sex when she could but was experiencing dyspareunia.

At the end of her second visit she informed me that she decided to have breast augmentation surgery. She did so after our third session, despite my cautioning her against it. She was spending a great deal of money shopping but was hiding her debts from her husband. She was having migraine and rebound headaches and was using, in my opinion, far too many medications. Her affair with a merchant began. She did not reveal for several sessions that the man was a business rival of her husband. The affair ran a four-month course. As soon as it was over, she became addicted to an opioid that she obtained through the Internet. Her life appeared to be a succession of impulsive, addictive, compulsive activities that routinely put herself and her marriage in jeopardy. After a brief recrudescence of the affair, she was able to end it because it was "crazy."

Linda's infidelity is part of a lifelong pattern of impulsive dangerous behaviors that she does not think through very clearly.

Infidelity can be a product of various forms of psychopathology as I hope Joy, Rocco, Frank, and Linda's marital rulebreaking indicate. In my experience, however, most cases are not simply due to a major psychopathology. The following is a more typical story which I have heard repeatedly from men and women. Is Kathy's infidelity sick? The patient gave permission to share her story (Levine & Stagno, 2001).

Gregarious but chronically sad, Kathy was clear and uncompromising about the moral turpitude and destructiveness of affairs. She had personally experienced their chaos in childhood from each parent's sexual meanderings. Her intense commitment to fidelity was repeatedly tested over many years by the many men who were attracted to her beauty. She reported that she was more often disgusted by men's disloyalty to their wives than complimented by their interest in her.

She had thought that she had married well, but soon recognized that she had made a colossal error of judgment. Her mistake was to excuse away her fiancé's lack of sexual interest in her during courtship. His sexual disinterest continued after the wedding. Within several weeks of their marriage, her husband became involved with a woman. Several years later, when he behaved inappropriately with a different woman, she learned of his earlier relationship. Her chronic low level anxiety and sadness which she carried from her troubled youth morphed into rage, depression, and suicidal ideation which brought her back to her psychotherapist.

When I met Kathy and her husband years later, they had four grade school children. Six months earlier, Kathy moved her husband out of the house after learning of his interest in a third sexual partner. Mutual gloom and tension characterized their contacts with each other as they tried to decide what to do with their marriage.

Kathy felt somewhat better from months of frank therapy discussions and using different medications for her anergic depression, and the couple decided to reunite because of their children. His silent sexual avoidance continued, but her ceaseless anger gradually became replaced by a sad acceptance of her husband's inability to be psychologically intimate and spontaneous with her. She resolved to spend her life asexually. This was not that difficult she claimed because she rarely recognized any sexual desire.

To get on with their lives they decided to remodel their home. Kathy was in charge of the project while her husband attended to his important job. The architect spent a lot of time overseeing the construction. Several months later after telling her much about his family life, he surprised her by declaring his love for her. She kindly informed him that she only wanted his friendship. For a month he did not mention the subject but she saw his yearning and eventually admitted to herself that she had become eager for his visits. When she nervously stopped his unexpected kiss, she experienced three days of nonstop genital excitement. When they next saw each other, she had no resistance. "Wondrous sex" began. She felt guilty between sexual encounters. A month later, after her husband commented on her apparent happiness ("New antidepressant?" he asked), he developed a wordless one-night sexual passion for her. She broke off the affair and immediately became depressed again. When she and her lover resumed five weeks later, she had no more guilt. Despite her SSRI, she remained suffused with desire and readily orgasmic. She no longer believed that she had to give up sexual pleasures while raising her children, assisting her husband with his business career, and caring for her chronically ill sister. Her felt need for psychotherapy diminished.

Looking at the load of psychiatric symptoms that Kathy carries and the duration of this burden, it is not difficult to conclude that she has a chronic psychiatric disorder. But her disorder per se does not explain her infidelity. Many good things have come to the family as a result of this new arrangement. The children again have a happy home, the wife supports her husband socially, they remain financially comfortable, the husband concentrates on his work, and, of course, the wife feels loved and satisfied with her sexual opportunities. The price she pays is periodic guilt. The price he pays is not apparent.

Marital or Sexual Unhappiness

Unhappiness in marriage is a powerful negative force in life. Without infidelity, this unhappiness can generate chronic sadness, worry, anxiety attacks, nagging thoughts, and addictions. Fidelity can be associated with a heavy price tag — a life that feels empty.

The psychiatric pendulum has shifted away from an interest in the psychosocial origins of depression and anxiety. We expect now to treat such states with biological therapies and pay only lip service to their psychosocial origins. Our current approach produces quite modest results (DePaulo, 2006; Gabbard & Freedman, 2006; Trivedi et al., 2006). Infidelity is not the cause of most depressions or anxiety states encountered in our practices, but it is shocking to realize how little most mental health professionals know about infidelity in their patients. They rarely even ask.

Human sexual desires cannot usually be suppressed for a lifetime. People devise numerous schemes for overcoming or compensating for their marital impediments. In the sexual sphere, these may involve pornography, strip clubs, message parlors, prostitutes, Internet chats, and liaisons with strangers, flings, and affairs. To employ these alternatives, people have to either not believe in fidelity, believe that they are not being unfaithful, feel guilty, outgrow their previous values, develop a strong sense of entitlement, or not think about it much. We should not forget, however, that many people respond to their lack of sexual happiness by shrugging their shoulders and turning their attention to other activities. Perhaps they never considered it important in the first place.

Youthful Romantic Ideals Prove to Be Mythical for Many

- We often hear that sex is about love. Frequently, it isn't; it is about the wish to have a sexual interaction.

- Extramarital sex can be a search for love, but its yield is low. It typically brings new private and interpersonal problems with it, which often put an end to the infidelity.

- Love should set the stage for a lifetime of sex. Many couples' love becomes prematurely companionate — that is, it becomes sexless despite their statements of love.

- Partner sex has the reputation for being incomparably better than solo sex. Many married people prefer masturbation.

- Sex within marriage has the potential to enable each partner to feel that he or she is loved and capable of loving. Many people feel hungry for love after sex.

The Therapist Can Be Part of a Marital Triangle

Some patients have long-term psychotherapy for the experience of psychological intimacy. They find an uncritical acceptance of and interest in their views, support for their ambitions, and answers to some of their questions about life processes. They often speak about the fixed limitations of their spouses. Some want to continue seeing the therapist well after their presenting complaints ameliorate because we seem to provide a substitute for what is missing at home. Eventually, we begin to think of ourselves as the third person in this patient's marriage. The patient settles for psychological intimacy with us. Their sex with us is only in their fantasies, which most hide from us. A therapist, however wonderful, cannot fulfill the role of a good spouse.

Few people outside our profession regard what we do as participating in a triangle of love. Triangles are spoken of with social opprobrium when psychological and sexual intimacy with someone else occurs. Therapists can be the safe third person in lieu of a lover. But the intimacy with a therapist can also make an unhappily married person realize that there is a better way to live. Ironically, psychotherapy may eventually lead to infidelity or divorce and those who are abandoned may come to view us with derision.

8. Love Is
Connection-Disconnection-Reconnection

In the early chapters I supplied words and concepts for the inchoate aspects of love. In the middle chapters I illuminated what I know about psychological intimacy and sexual desire, the vital pathways for obtaining and maintaining loving feelings. In the previous chapter on infidelity, I emphasized how unsatisfying love can be for some people when their ambitions to love and be loved are thwarted. In this final chapter I illustrate how the contents of the first seven chapters are revealed whenever an individual patient or a couple is willing to share their struggles with love. Over time, love is a process of fluctuating degrees of emotional connection.

A Collusion of Silence

I began the book with a question: What is love? Most mental health professionals collude with individuals and social institutions by pretending that we know what love is. Others in our society function under a pact that instructs people and their institutions not to speak about love with uncertainty and not to admit to any confusion about the topic. The price of breaking the pact is to be dismissed as being in a state of extreme distress or occasionally as being mentally ill. This is, of course, where we mental health professionals come in. It is easy to find writers of every ilk, including great ones, who invoke love as though their readers will know exactly what the word means. I have not been one of their trusting readers of late. As a younger psychiatrist, when I felt less certain about the nature of love, I thought I had not lived long enough to understand and I worried that I was singularly unable to comprehend its meaning. I feel a lot better now.

Love Used to Be Largely Intuitive

Not only do I no longer assume that love is actually one thing, I recognize that most of what we think we know about love is intuitive. We don't really have words for what we know. Our knowledge resides within us in preverbal forms. I am not sure about when and how we acquire our convictions about love, but most people seem to have them when life does not go well for them or someone they care about.

The nine nouns of love represent what used to be largely intuitive or partially understood about love. During this recapitulation of the different elements that constitute love, please note three things: (1) One concept of love easily merges into the next one. (2) Each of the nine nouns implies an action process, or love as a verb. (3) Each person's use of the word has changeable or unstable meanings.

1. Love is a grand, idealized, culturally reinforced *ambition* (deRougement, 1963).

2. Love is the label for the *arrangement* that people make with each other. During courtship, the most obvious process of making this arrangement, individuals privately weigh various aspects of the other person to determine whether the relationship will prove to be a good deal over time. When it is judged to be a good one, each person begins to realize the lofty ambitions of love. Love is then said to exist.

3. This love gives birth to a tenacious bond. Clinicians use the term *attachment* for this bond (Bowlby, 1989). Either term is preferred by most people over the economic or legal term, *contract*. Love is, nonetheless, a contract to be a couple. The terms of the contract are rarely spelled out in full (Sager et al., 1971). They tend to be discovered over time as two people happen upon their disagreements and find that they have differing expectations for their relationship.

4. Love is the arrangement after it has been imbued with sacred, moral, and legal implications. Society is deeply involved with love. It insists upon ritualizing the recog-

nition of the new unit through religious or secular ceremonies of *moral commitment*. The ceremonies declare another meaning of love: the mutual obligations to work hard to realize love's lofty ideals. The ceremonies, however, give few clues as to how this work is to be accomplished or about the disappointments with which the individuals will need to cope (Viorst, 1986).

5. Love is the intrapsychic private conscious and unconscious work required to live up to love's moral implications. The work of love is a *self-management process* that can last a lifetime.

6. Love is a *force in nature* that has its way with us throughout the life cycle. It is something far larger than what is happening in individual lives. Love challenges us to abide in a supportive manner even as we grow older and care for each other in diminished states. Both the charm of new love and the caregiving of love's end processes are part of nature. This instinctual life force has always proven difficult to capture in words.

7. Love is an *ever-changing pattern of emotions* experienced with and about another person. Love is most commonly thought of in terms of its extensive emotional potentials — intense suffering, comforting stabilities, and joyful highs. The emotional aspects of love are frequently oversimplified by representing love as a unique feeling state.

At any particular moment, love as emotion is an array of feelings rather than a universal affective commonality.

8. Love is a socially perpetuated *illusion*. The functions and processes of love are too central to our lives for us to ever be totally free of those illusions, which are indeed, necessary for us to fall in love, to be in love, and to stay in love (Levine, 1998). Denial of the illusory aspects of love prevents us from understanding love's richness (Kernberg, 1995). Love, of course, is not entirely an illusion but neither is it what both human beings and the culture at times make it out to be. Clinicians who try to learn about a person's love relationship quickly may encounter another meaning of love — don't go there! The details of personal love are experienced as a subject to be concealed.

9. Love is a *stop sign*. Clinicians often have reasons to inquire about a person's relationship when we are baffled about why certain behaviors are tolerated. We then may discover that although our questions are reasonable and relevant to the suffering at hand, the only answer is "because I love him (her)." This phrase is a euphemism for the unwillingness to explain the answer to the therapist or for the disinclination to personally consider the topic. This well-disguised command to stop reminds us that what we think, feel, and do in relationship to our lover or spouse is simply a very private matter. Even a psychoanalyst who conducts therapy with a patient five days a week cannot expect to learn about all of

the motives and considerations that have gone into creating
and maintaining the patient's social circumstances.

The Nouns of Love Are Merely Snapshots of the Verbs of Love

These nine nouns of love, however illuminating, are ultimately an
insufficient explanation of love. Collectively, they serve to clarify
that love is a continuous process of sharing some aspects of the
self with another. Love is a process of connection. Its nouns are
merely snapshots of an ever-moving process. Many key moments
in this process are highly stimulating in affective terms. Love
sometimes brings joy, sexual desire, contentment, disappointment, competitiveness, jealousy, rage, grief, helplessness, confusion, and hopelessness. While the transient positive emotions are
the most celebrated aspects of love, therapists cannot afford to
confuse these emotions with love itself. If we watched a movie of
two people having exciting sex, we would not insist that the picture captured all there is to know about sex. We also recognize
that, like sex, many of love's processes remain invisible. Fromm
once wrote that there is no such thing as love because it is only an
abstraction. He felt that only acts of love existed — that is, activities of caring for, knowing, responding, affirming, and enjoying
the person (Fromm, 1976).

The Illumination of Unhappiness

The nouns of love are extremely helpful in understanding the temporary and chronic unhappiness that can occur in love relationships. Patients bring their relationships to us when they have evidence that they are not experiencing anything close to love's ideals. Their partners are not accompanying, assisting, emotionally stabilizing, or sufficiently enriching their lives. They have not felt much pleasure, interest, or sexual desire for their partners lately. Psychological intimacy is rarely attained. The deal that they originally made is now perceived to have evolved into a distinctly bad one. The partner is unfair, refuses to see the world in a compatible way, and too frequently provokes profound disappointment. Cynicism about the partner and love in general mounts because the partner is perceived as having reneged on the contract. So many negative experiences with the partner have occurred by the time the person seeks our assistance that he or she can no longer maintain the internal idealized image of the partner. Regardless of what such patients tell us, ending the arrangement is a serious consideration at that point.

Many patients think that their intense anger and deep disappointment have propelled them to a position that is the opposite of love. They may say that they have fallen out of love. Intense anger, which is sometimes labeled *hatred*, is, however, only a step toward the opposite of love, which is indifference. Intense anger can be a strong magnet that binds two people together and makes the letting go of the partner more difficult.

Even in the face of their bitterness and disappointment, those who seek our services often clearly state that they still have love for their partner. They mean that they still feel a moral commitment to them. The bond is still there because of their promise to make it last, because they have shared these years of their lives, because they maintain hope that the partner can eventually overcome his or her deficiencies, and because, aside from the problem being brought to us, other aspects of the marriage may still be a good deal. They seek help because they fear that they may one day grow to be indifferent toward their partners.

"I love him, doctor, but I am not in love with him": this often means that, "I'm still committed to him, but I have no pleasure or interest in him any longer. I view him far more realistically now." Such relationships often are described as empty (Sternberg, 1988). When such a couple arrives for conjoint work, the therapist is fortunate if their statement of moral commitment is sincere and they are genuinely willing to invest in an affectively powerful process that may lead to better behaviors, greater genuineness, and a change in attitude toward the partner. The therapeutic goal is to facilitate the recurrence of psychological and sexual intimacies within the union.

Love's Affects Come and Go

New love, threatened love, and lost love make it clear that this complex thing and process abides in close proximity to affective intensity. Love relationships can instantly provoke positive and negative emotional upheavals. When we watch anyone who is falling in love, in the process of breaking up, or dealing with the threatened or actual death of a partner, we readily discern strong affects. When the processes of love work well, ironically, love's intensities recede. In some individuals, the emotions of love fade beyond the person's capacity to realize that they are present. These individuals can readily overlook the emotionally stabilizing effects of their relationship when they worry about the lack of clear pleasure, genuine interest, and sexual desire for the partner. Their love has lost the emotional connection upon which they depend to recognize love. They want the feelings back. Many report that they feel bored. The culture's silence about the ordinariness of this state of love makes them wonder whether they still love their partner.

The affective side of love and the sense of connection often have many ups and downs. It is not necessarily a serious pathological state when a spouse cannot recognize much emotional intensity. It would make a lot of people's lives easier if they understood this. When one partner does not understand and the other tries to explain his or her lack of strong positive emotions, there is a great risk that the partner will only hear, "I don't love you!" This perception can stimulate the specter of abandonment, which in modern terms generally means anxiety attacks. Lurking behind such misperception is the expectation that "I should continue to be a source of pleasure for you; you should think of me in wonderful terms." The fading emotions of love occasionally can be revived by imagining the loss of the partner, witnessing someone flirt with the partner, being on one's own for several days, or experiencing the partner's angry withdrawal. These experiences may reassure the person that the emotions of connection are present and create a temporary renewed appreciation. Connection, disconnection, reconnection is the relationship process that the culture is loathe to acknowledge. Connection, disconnection, and reconnection, however, are what many therapists hear about many hours per day.

An "Infidelity" Crisis

Fifteen months before the following material was written, Karl, age 61, and Margaret, age 58, had the first of 12 sessions to deal with Karl's years of surreptitious chatting on the Internet. These behaviors originally arose at age 53, when Margaret went out of state to care for her declining father soon after their last child left for college. Later, her father came to live with them. Karl's previous secretive sexual behaviors had consisted of occasional visits to strip clubs. He gave up that activity when he discovered cybersex. His extramarital sex behaviors thereafter consisted of mutual masturbation while chatting on the computer and the telephone. Occasionally these activities made use of a computer-linked camera. They took place at work, on a cell phone in his car, and at his home. He met in person two of the women he chatted with over the years. (He had not told Margaret about Darlene, the more recent of the women with whom he had sex play four times in his car.) Previous attempts at psychotherapy and an SSRI had made no significant impact on what Karl called his sexual addictions.

Karl felt that these extramarital activities enabled him to feel that he was powerfully in control, seductive, and charmingly empathetic — he felt this way about all 12 of the women. "I became the ladies man that I never was." In his 20s, he had maintained an intense unrequited love for two years, without so much as a kiss. Karl said that in the real world he rarely felt respected, had poor self-confidence, felt disconnected from people (even those who loved him), and knew himself to be a passive-aggressive depressive man. Margaret discovered his unacceptable behavior three times. Each time Karl promised her that he would not further jeopardize the marriage or hurt her with his infidelities.

The couple kept a daily journal during our sessions. I encouraged them to keep talking about their histories, their subjectivities, and to tell each other things that they had previously withheld from one another. After Karl lost his erection one night, Margaret's inquiries led to the revelation of the four episodes of sex in the car. Margaret understood Karl's hesitance to speak of his internal life. When he tried and succeeded at it, she responded by loving him more, even though she was disappointed by what he was telling her. Their talks and our sessions were highly emotional. We were all pleased with the results. Karl stayed away from all the problematic behaviors for nine months. They were quite happy with one another and continued a regular and more arousing sexual life together than they had in several decades.

Six months ago, Darlene called to tell him she was divorcing. Karl informed Margaret that evening of the call. Margaret was grateful for his revelation but was hurt that he did not tell Darlene not to call again. Margaret remembered this as a brief incident that did not interfere with their loving sexual relationship. The call, however, stimulated Karl in ways that led to a crisis four months later. Karl perceived his wife's initial anger and felt that she disapproved of how long he spoke to Darlene, but Darlene's continuing interest in him stirred and pleased him. Within a week, he began to privately debate whether he should view soft porn sites again. After resisting for another week, he returned to looking at free computer images of breasts. After doing this periodically for several weeks, he desired to reacquaint himself with how he felt being a part of other women's lives. He tried to resist by reminding himself how controlled he used to feel by that desire. Within several days, he began to reread the e-mail communications with the 12 women. He again saw how sensitive, romantic, and poetic he had been. After Margaret learned about the e-mails, he decided on his own to destroy them. Margaret's anger, disappointment, and despair over the e-mails precipitated the crisis.

Karl came to see me alone at first. One week later we had a conjoint session. Each session had a déjà vu quality for me. I asked them to write about their current dilemmas (Scheinkman, 2005). They complied over the next 36 hours. As an expression of my gratitude for agreeing to have me write about them (Levine & Stagno, 2001), I sent them a nearly final version of Chapter 1 of this book. I thought it might help them understand their emotional storms.

MARGARET'S SUMMARY ON THE DAY OF OUR SESSION

Karl and I have had 37 years of life experience together. We have raised children, cared for elderly parents, become grandparents, and have had a wealth of shared life history. However, I am married to a man who has not respected or honored his marriage vows for at least nine years. His actions have not shown respect, honor, or love for me. I am married to a man who has shown a form of emotional abuse by committing his actions of unfaithfulness and then becoming angry, hostile, or belittling as his guilt increases (also at such times telling me that he can't say he loves me; he just "doesn't know what love really is"). This is followed by confession and a "commitment" to not hurt me, and efforts to convince me that he is working hard to put his life of unfaithfulness behind him. All the while he continues his Internet sex chat, phone sex, and "relationships" with women online, some of which spill into the real world as he meets various women in person. Karl is a very good liar, and each time he has committed "to not participating in any action that would jeopardize our marriage" and his "proving" to me that he cares enough for me not to be unfaithful (once for two years, once for six years, and this last time for six months), I have believed him fully and have loved him all the more for the effort

that I felt it must have taken for him to do such hard work and to
be so fully committed to our marriage. I have given myself to him
emotionally and physically with love and respect during these periods
when I believed Karl was not cheating. Then his pattern has been to
pull the rug out from under me and to confess to having continued his
relationships all along. This third time of the "cheat and lie; repent"
cycle has caused me to lose all trust in my husband and to have the
need to distance myself from him emotionally and physically. Karl is a
cheater (my definition: Karl is a man who has emotional relationships
with other women; often these lead to sex) and a liar.

So.... what to do? Do I ask him to leave? Do we have a "marriage
of convenience," one in which we live together on a superficial basis,
leading separate emotional lives; thus sparing Karl shame and sparing
his children unnecessary sorrow? Do I once again try (how? why?) to
open myself emotionally or physically to my husband?

Karl's Account of His Dilemmas

I'll list my dilemmas just as Margaret has done. I think it will be
harder for me as she is the aggrieved party, and I am the guilty one.
Margaret's dilemmas seem at times clearer and more easily stated.

My biggest dilemma is: How can I become the man that I am
not? Early on we decided not to dwell on the "what's wrong with
Karl?" kinds of questions. The solution to resolve the problem was
no big mystery. I didn't need drugs to stop the behavior, and I didn't
need to rehash every childhood hurt, trauma, and disappointment. If I
could establish true psychological intimacy with my wife then the real
or pseudo needs seemingly satisfied by my infidelities would diminish
and disappear.

We practiced psychological intimacy as best we could. But I
didn't do it well enough. I couldn't articulate many of my discon-
tents or couldn't articulate them well enough. Still, we practiced it as
best we could for almost a year. Psychological intimacy broke down
sometime in the fall when "the lady in the car" called to say hello. It

was an awkward call, but I can't deny that it was pleasing to my ego at the same time. True to our "no secrets" pact, I told Margaret of the call that evening. Margaret was furious and demanded that if she ever called again I should tell her in no uncertain terms that she should not call again. Margaret's attitude angered me, but I kept it to myself. It was like my mother catching me in an act of masturbation (which actually happened) and telling me that I shouldn't do it again.

I've been a passive-aggressive person all my life. Instead of confronting Margaret about her mandate to me, I kept quiet, but a month or so later I started visiting a few soft porn sites which I hadn't visited in a year. Soon I was opening other forbidden doors as well — I reread old e-mails and wondered about some of these women. I made no attempt to contact any of them. When rereading these e-mails, I remembered feeling angry that Margaret insisted, when my chatting and infidelity was discovered a second time, that I write each woman immediately and tell them that I would from this day forward have no contact with them. I said nothing to Margaret about my resentment at the time.

So here is another dilemma: How do I express to a woman who has every right to be angry with me that I am still angry with her? Had I been able to be the man I am not, I could have expressed my anger immediately and perhaps prevented a return to my secret Internet activity.

How do two people really ever get it *all* out in the open? I am shy and unassertive with people in general and with my wife in particular. I've felt a release from inhibitions in anonymous cybersex that I've never felt in real life. Another dilemma: How do I accept the fact that sex and intimacy in the real world will never be as uninhibited as they are in the cyber world and accept the real world as good enough? I have already made the decision not to go back to the cyberworld for sex, but the temptation and opportunity will always be there. So the dilemma is how does someone with impulse control problems ever feel confident that his old ways will not return. How does a passive-aggressive person like myself find a better way to "thumb his nose" at the world when the need arises?

I do have a depressive personality. Margaret does not. My dilemma is how to live in her world where she is comfortable and I am a stranger. I know the type of man she would want me to be — not perfect by any means, but far different from the man she is married to at the moment. Psychological intimacy is supposed to bridge that gap, but our attempt at it hasn't worked yet.

The dilemma is what to do now? Stay the course and try harder or steer another course? The latter is very frightening because what I dread the most is Margaret and Karl becoming "disinterested" in each other.

KARL'S LETTER TO MARGARET AFTER WRITING TO ME

This is what I know for sure. My actions, my errors, my decisions, my deceit, my arrogance, my selfishness, my failures have caused you great emotional harm and pain. You see me as a cheat and a liar and a person unwilling to honor my marriage vows and unable to support and love you in a meaningful and necessary way. You question whether I have any desire to restore our relationship; or whether you have any desire to restore the relationship, and risk being hurt again by someone whose actions have destroyed your ability to trust. My actions and failures have caused this harm and pain. I am so sorry this has happened. There is nothing insincere about my remorse. If I am getting any sadistic pleasure from this (which has occurred to you), then I am the most evil of men.

Levine said that the opposite of love is not hate but detachment and disinterest. He had a better word but I can't remember it. Getting to that point is what frightens me the most. But I am not at the point of detachment and disinterest, or even close, and I don't believe you are either. The pains we are going through tell me that there is real and genuine love between us. That gives me hope.

We can find a way out of this. We should find a way out if it. Levine can help us. Psychological intimacy is the key to our way out,

and we gave it a good try the last time but fell short. I didn't trust the
process as much as I needed to in order to make it work.

I want to reassure you. I want to reach out to you. We aren't ready
to reach out sexually. I miss being able to hold you. And now this is
what I hope for ... with some but not total assurance. We will talk
more. Some of your pain will subside. There will be no winner and
loser in this process. Maybe there will be a real breakthrough, a really
hallelujah moment. We will accept each other, frailties and all. Things
will seem in perspective again.

THE COUPLE'S RESPONSES TO CHAPTER 1

Karl: Yes it helped to read the chapter. Margaret and I grew up believing in the worthwhile nature of love. I don't want to be told that love
can die. I want it to be eternal, changing, evolving, diminishing only
to be reborn in a different form. You never mention the possibility of
love dying in this chapter. I think I like that.

Margaret: The entire chapter gave such clear guidance about the complexity of "this thing called love." What resonated most was the love
as an ambition. What you wrote expresses what I most want: respect,
behavioral reliability, enjoyment of one another, sexual pleasure, fidelity, psychological intimacy, and a comfortable balance of individuality
and couplehood. This and the next phrasing of the ambition is what
I want. As Karl and I begin to connect again, we will be working
toward this ideation as most important. Thank you for the gift of sharing chapter 1.

WHAT IS THE THERAPIST TO DO?

I try never to assume that I have the full story. For many reasons I don't think anyone can tell the whole story. In part this is
because the couple does not know it. I am generally pleased as

more of the story unfolds over time. It is often my illusion that clinical material speaks for itself, particularly over time, but I grudgingly admit that clinical material speaks differently to each of us.

Here were my initial impressions:

1. A middle-aged couple, who would naturally be in a phase of less emotional intensity/more stability, greatly improved their nonsexual and sexual lives through frank discussions about their subjectivities.

2. When they moved her father into their home this wisely ended their periodic separations.

3. Karl's discovery of a solution for his masculine inadequacy through the Internet initially gave him the illusion of really knowing other women without meeting them. Such infidelity is based on limiting the scope of a relationship.

4. The couple cared for and about each other reasonably well for decades despite his difficulties. They continue to seem connected to one another.

5. Margaret feels strongly that he should always sincerely represent himself as loving her, that he should never give in to his normal, natural curiosity about other women, because she has not given in to the same curiosity about other men, and that she should be his exclusive sexual partner.

6. She does not seem to want to banish him, create an empty marriage, or feel like she is a fool again.

7. I don't understand this crisis well enough. Did he do or feel something else? Is Margaret's intensity derived primarily from the past, was she was deliberately trying something dramatic to extinguish Karl's future extramarital temptations, or am I missing something?

8. Do I need to help them accept the ordinary complexity of love, Karl's characterologic limitations, and Margaret's emotional tendency to make all of her marriage rest upon one issue?

9. They think I know what to do about their dilemmas. Of course, I don't.

Karl returned in 10 days with a note from Margaret saying that she has allowed him back into the bed. She was allowing hand-holding only. Karl is ready for more but she could not tolerate anything else. She said that this was not vindictiveness; it simply protects her until she can trust him again. They are having lots of good conversations and enjoying each other's company. She is grateful for the time and space he is giving her. Karl said that he feels as if there is a 2×6 plank separating them in bed.

When Karl tried to reveal his additional dilemmas, he interrupted his descriptions with self-castigations such as, "When will I grow up? When will I become a mature man? When will I accept that I simply must give up my pleasures with other women?" I reminded him that this self-scolding was familiar to me; I remembered that it had not helped him in the past. "Karl, your exhortations do not sound like a plan to me." He opened a book that described masturbation as a declaration of freedom from the constrictions of parents and saw that his infidelities were a declaration of freedom from Margaret. While he resonated with this strongly, he said he did not understand what it was he was rebelling against.

He was soon explaining how much he had learned from these 12 women. They told him about their sexual patterns, they made wonderful, explosive orgasmic sounds over the phone, they taught him that women really could enjoy breast stimulation, and that they wanted him to see their breasts. We agreed that he had become confident that he now could seduce a woman to have sex with him. "Should Margaret die," I said, "you are not likely to repeat the humiliation of your early twenties." I told him that he was now at an attractive phase of his life — a neatly dressed, well-spoken, physically healthy man with a stable job. If he walked with a cane, on the other hand, he would be less attractive to many women. "You are not yet decrepit." But now that he knew that he could attract women, he had to recognize that he was free to choose whether to pursue other women. As I told him when he first came to me, he does not have to hide irresponsibly behind obscuring concepts such as compulsions, addictions, and poor impulse control. He knows why he does this. It is no longer because he feels insecure about his Romeo capacities. It is because it is pleasing to him and he does not like to be restricted.

He then revealed that Margaret had placed so much of her body off limits to him after the courtship. During orgasm, she would never make sounds or allow him to make a sound lest the children or her father hear. He never told her of his breast hunger. He immediately interrupted his revelation to castigate himself as immature because of this. I said that I had heard of breast fascination somewhere before (Acocella, 2006). He laughed. We turned to how difficult it would be to describe this hunger to Margaret who has always maintained that her breasts were too sensitive to be touched during lovemaking. "Margaret thinks our sex life has been so good and …. It has been, but … it is quiet missionary sex. We have not had oral sex in a very long time." He recalled his pleasure in exciting Darlene at her breasts. He added that he never loved Darlene but was grateful for what had transpired sexually between them.

Karl then revealed that Darlene's call to him occurred on his birthday. It was obvious to him that she was still attracted to him. One week later Margaret casually told him she loved him. Rather than saying something in kind, he asked her if she wanted some tea. She was crushed. She soon asked him about the chat rooms. One tense week later, he confessed about the e-mails.

Ten days after meeting Karl, the couple returned in a cheerful mood. Margaret calmly discussed Karl's breast hunger. She explained that she has long devoted herself to helping him to feel more masculine and that she withdrew her body for fore-play, in part, because of how uncomfortable he had often seemed in touching her long ago. This theme, sex is interactive while everyone has his or her I-am-the-victim-of-my-partner perspec-tive, was thoroughly discussed. Karl cried while saying he only wanted to be with Margaret but was afraid that he would slip again in the future. I said it was a shame that Margaret had not had a wonderful extramarital experience that she could call up whenever life became frustrating for her. She smiled and said that she could understand Karl's memories and that he should not keep his longings secret. "Karl can come to me with his sex-ual frustration." I gave them a suggestion about stimulating her armpit prior to her breast. This pleased both of them. I added that I doubted that her breasts still had the extreme sensitivity that they possessed when she was much younger. We scheduled our next visit at a longer interval.

Several days later, Margaret e-mailed me to say, "Your arm suggestion to us was most successful, fun, and fulfilling. Karl called it splendid."

I hope you can see that my approach to therapy consists of understanding what is being said and sensing what is not said. I try to give a voice to each of my patients and to clarify their indi-vidual and relationship dilemmas. I no longer experience most relationship situations as terribly unique, but I do find most of them to be complex. I do not present myself as actually hav-ing solutions to most problems that people bring to me. I try to judiciously use my knowledge of love's processes, psychological intimacy, and sexual desire to educate and inspire. I do not shy away from sexual concerns, complaints, and dilemmas. I carefully describe and embrace the couples' dilemmas with, I hope, kindness, occasional humor, and mild optimism. I have great respect for the inevitability of life's conundrums. Over the years I have found that my respect somehow provides my patients with hope, energy, and an evolving perspective on the nature of love. In this manner, through my style of connection, I am providing love for my patients.

References

Ackerman, D. (1994). *The natural history of love.* New York: Random House.

Acocella, J. (2006, March 20). The girls next door. *The New Yorker,* 144–148.

Alberoni, F. (1983). *Falling in love: A revolutionary way of thinking about a universal experience.* (L. Venuti, Trans.). New York: Random House.

American Psychiatric Association. (1980). *Diagnostic and statistical manual of mental disorders* (3rd ed. rev.). Washington, D.C.: Author.

American Psychiatric Association. (2000). *Diagnostic and statistical manual of mental disorders* (text rev.). Washington, D.C.: Author.

American Psychiatric Association, Ethics Committee. (2005). *Principles of ethics and professionalism in psychiatry.* Washington, D.C.: Author.

Aron, E. N., & Aron, A. (1996). Love and the expansion of the self: The state of the model. *Personal Relationships, 3,* 45–58.

Aron, A., Fisher, H., Mashek, D. J., Strong, G., Haifang, L., & Brown, L. L. (2005). Reward, motivation, and emotion systems associated with early stage intense romantic love. *Journal of Neurophysiology, 94,* 327–337.

Barlow, A., Duncan, S., James, G., & Park, A. (2001). Just a piece of paper: Marriage and co-habitation. In A. Park, J. Curtis, L. Thompson, C. Jarvis, C. Bromley, & N. Stratford (Eds.), *British social attitudes*: 18th report (pp. 29–58). London: Sage.

Bartels, A., & Zeki, S. (2000). The neural basis of romantic love. *Neuroreport, 11* (17): 3829-34.

Basson, R. (2000). The female sexual response: A different model. *Journal of Sex and Marital Therapy, 26*(1), 51–65.

Basson, R. (2001). Human sex response cycles. *Journal of Sex and Marital Therapy, 27*(1), 33–43.

Basson, R. (2006). Sexual desire and arousal disorders in women. *New England Journal of Medicine, 354*(14), 1497–1506.

Basson, R., McInnes, R., Smith, M. D., Hodgson, G., & Koppiker, N. (2002). Efficacy and safety of sildenafil citrate with sexual dysfunction associated with female sexual arousal disorder. *Journal of Women's Health: Gender Based Medicine, 11*(4), 367–377.

Baumeister, R. F., & Bratslavsky, E. (1999). Passion, intimacy, and time: Passionate love as a function of change in intimacy. *Personality and Social Psychology Review, 3*(1), 49–67.

Bergmann, J. R. (1993). *Discreet indiscretions: The social organization of gossip.* New York: Aldine de Gruyter.

Bergner, R. M. (2002). Sexual compulsion as an attempted recovery from degradation. *Journal of Sex and Marital Therapy, 28,* 373–387.

Bergner, R. M. (2005). Lovemaking as a ceremony of accreditation. *Journal of Sex and Marital Therapy, 31*(5), 425–432.

Bergner, R. M., & Bridges, A. J. (2002). The significance of heavy pornography involvement for romantic partners: Research and clinical implications. *Journal of Sex and Marital Therapy, 28,* 193–206.

Betzig, L. (1989). Causes of conjugal dissolution: A cross-cultural study. *Current Anthropology, 30,* 654–676.

Bowlby, J. (1989). *The making and breaking of affectional bonds.* London: Routledge.

Brezsnyak, M., & Whisman, M. A. (2004). Sexual desire and relationship functioning: The effects of marital satisfaction and power. *Journal of Sex and Marital Therapy, 30*(3), 199–217.

Brown, E. (1999). *Patterns of infidelity and affairs: A guide to working through the repercussions of infidelity.* New York: Jossey-Bass.

Butler, R. N. (1975). Psychiatry and the elderly: An overview. *American Journal of Psychiatry, 132*(9), 893–900.

Clement, U. (2002). Sex in long-term relationships: A systemic approach to sexual desire problems. *Archives of Sexual Behavior, 31*(3), 241–246.

Cooper, A. S., & Marcus, D. I. (2003). Men who lose control of their sexual behavior. In S. B. Levine, C. B. Risen, & S. E. Althof (Eds.), *The handbook of clinical sexuality for mental health professionals* (pp. 311–332). New York: Brunner/Routledge.

Crews, D. (1998). The evolutionary antecedents to love. *Psychoneuroendocrinology, 23,* 751–764.

Davis, S. R., Davison, S. L., Donath, S., & Bell, R. J. (2005). Circulating androgen levels and self-reported sexual function in women. *Journal of the American Medical Association, 294*(1), 91–96.

de Botton, A. (1993). *On Love*. New York: Grove Press.

Dennerstein, L. (2003). The sexual impact of menopause. In S. B. Levine, C. B. Risen, S. E. Althof (Eds.), *The handbook of clinical sexuality for mental health professionals* (pp. 187-198). New York: Brunner/Routledge.

Dennerstein, L., Smith, A., Morse, C., & Burger, H. (1994). Sexuality in menopause. *Journal of Psychosomatic Obstetrics and Gynecology*, 15, 59–66.

DePaulo, J. R. (2006). Bipolar disorder treatment: An evidence-based reality check (editorial). *American Journal of Psychiatry*, 163(2), 175–176.

deRougement, J. (1963). *Love declared: Essays on the myths of love*. New York: Pantheon.

Donnellan, M. B., Larsen-Rife, D., & Conger, R. D. (2005). Personality, family history, and competence in early adult romantic relationships. *Journal of Personality and Social Psychology*, 88(3), 562–576.

Duncombe, J., Harrison, K., Allan, G., & Marsden, D. (Eds.). (2004). *The state of affairs: Explorations in infidelity and commitment*. Mahwah, NJ: Erlbaum.

Engelhardt, H. T. (1974). The disease of masturbation: Values and the concept of disease. *Journal of History of Medicine*, 48(2), 234–248.

Erikson, E. H. (1963). *Childhood and Society*. New York: Norton. (Second Edition).

Esch, T., & Stefano, G. B. (2005). The neurobiology of love. *Neuroendocrinology Letters, 26(3), 175–192*.

Everaerd, W., Laan, E. T. M., Both, S., & Van Der Velde, J. (2000). Female sexuality. In M. F. Szuchman LT (Ed.), *Psychological perspectives in human sexuality* (pp. 101–146). New York: Wiley.

Faulkner, S. L. (2003). Good girl or flirt girl: Latinas' definition of sex and sexual relationships. *Hispanic Journal of Behavioral Science*, 25, 174–200.

Federman, D. D. (2006). The biology of human sex differences. *The New England Journal of Medicine*, 354(14), 1507–1514.

Feldman, H. A., Goldstein, I., Hatzichristou, D.G., Krane, R. J., & McKinlay, J. B. (1994). Impotence and its medical and psychological correlates: Results of the Massachusetts Male Aging Study. *Journal of Urology*, 151, 54–61.

Fitcham, F. D., Paleari, F. G., & Regalia, C. (2002). Forgiveness in marriage: The role of relationship quality, attributions, and empathy. *Personal Relationships*, 9, 27–37.

Frank, K. (2005). Exploring the motivations and fantasies of strip club customers in relation to legal regulations. *Archives of Sexual Behavior*, 34(5), 487–504.

Freud, S. (1953). Three essays on the theory of sexuality. In J. Strachey (Ed. and Trans.), *The standard edition of the complete psychological works of Sigmund Freud* (Vol. 7, pp. 123–143). London: Hogarth Press. (Original work published 1905)

Freud, S. (1957). On the universal tendency to debasement in the sphere of love. In J. Strachey (Ed. and Trans.), *The standard edition of the complete psychological works of Sigmund Freud* (Vol. 11, pp. 177–190). London: Hogarth Press. (Original work published 1912)

Fromm, E. (1954). *The art of loving: An inquiry into the nature of love.* New York: Harper & Row.

Fromm, E. (1976). Having and being in daily experience. In *To have or to be?* (pp. 44–47). New York: Continuum.

Gabbard, G. O. (1998). Commentary on paper by Jody Messler Davis. *Psychoanalytic Dialogues, 8,* 781–791.

Gabbard, G. O., & Freedman, R. (2006). Psychotherapy in the journal: What's missing. *American Journal of Psychiatry, 163*(2), 182–184.

Gilligan, C. (1993). *In a different voice: Psychological theory and women's development.* Cambridge, MA: Harvard University Press.

Gilligan, C. (2003). *The birth of pleasure: A new map of love.* New York: Vintage Books.

Goldstein, I., Lue, T. F., Padma-Nathan, H., Rosen, R. C., Speers, W. C. et al. (1998). Oral sildenafil in the treatment of erectile dysfunction. *New England Journal of Medicine, 338*(20), 1397–1404.

Gordon, K., Baucom, D., & Synder, D. (2004). An integrative intervention for promoting recovery from extramarital affairs. *Journal of Marital and Family Therapy, 30,* 212–231.

Gottlieb, L. (2006, March). How do I love thee? *Atlantic Monthly, 297,* 58–71.

Gottman, J. M. (1998). Psychology and the study of marital processes. *Annual Review of Psychology, 49,* 169–197.

Gottman, J. M., & Katz, L. F. (1989). The effects of marital discord on young children's peer interactions and health. *Developmental Psychology, 25,* 373–381.

Gottman, J. M., & Krokoff, L. J. (1989). The relationship between marital interaction and marital satisfaction: A longitudinal view. *Journal of Consulting and Clinical Psychology, 57,* 47–52.

Greer, G. (1991). *The change: Women, aging, and the menopause.* New York: Knopf.

Hatfield, E., & Rapson, R. L. (1993). *Love, sex, and intimacy: Their psychology, biology, and history.* New York: HarperCollins.

Herdt, G., & McClintock, M. (2000). The magical age of 10. *Archives of Sexual Behavior, 29*(6), 587–606.

Insel, T. R. (2006). Beyond efficacy: The STAR-D trial (editorial). *American Journal of Psychiatry, 163*(1), 5–7.

Jankowiak, W. R., & Fisher, E. F. (1992). A cross-cultural perspective on romantic love. *Ethnology, 31,* 149–155.

Jordan, J. V. (1989). *Relational development: Therapeutic implications of empathy and shame*. Wellesley, MA: Stone Center.

Kaplan, H.S. (1976). Towards a Rational Classification of the Sexual Dysfunctions. *Journal of Sexual and Marital Therapy*, 2(2), 83-84.

Kaplan, H. S. (1977). *Sexual desire disorders and other new concepts and techniques of sex therapy*. New York: Brunner/Mazel.

Kernberg, O. (1995). *Love relations: Normal and pathological*. New Haven, CT: Yale University Press.

Kipnis, L. (2004). *Against love: A polemic*. New York: Vintage Books.

Kontula, O., & Haavio-Mannila, E. (2004). Renaissance of romanticism in the era of increasing individualism. In J. Duncombe, K. Harrison, G. Allan, & D. Marsden (Eds.), *The state of affairs: Explorations in infidelity and commitment* (pp. 79–102). Mahwah, NJ: Erlbaum.

Korpelainen, J. T., Hiltunen, P., & Myllyla, V. V. (1998). Moclobemide-induced hypersexuality in patients with stroke and Parkinson's disease. *Clinical Neuropharmacology*, 21, 251–254.

Krakauer, J. (2003). *Under the banner of heaven: A story of violent faith*. New York: Anchor.

Langstrom, N., & Hanson, R. K. (2006). High rates of sexual behavior in the general population: Correlates and predictors. *Archives of Sexual Behavior*, 35(1), 37–52.

Lear, J. (1990). *Love and its place in nature: A philosophical interpretation of Freudian psychoanalysis*. New York: Farrar, Straus & Giroux.

Lee, J. A. (1988). Love-styles. In M. L. Barnes (Ed.), *The psychology of love* (pp. 38–67). New Haven, CT: Yale University Press.

Levine, S. B. (1997). Sexual identity developing. In S. B. Levine (Ed.), *Solving common sexual problems*. Northvale, NJ: Jason Aronson.

Levine, S. B. (1998). *Sexuality in mid-life*. New York: Plenum.

Levine, S. B. (1999). Male heterosexuality. In R.C. Friedman & J. I. Downey (Eds.), *Masculinity and sexuality* (pp. 29–54). Washington, D.C.: American Psychiatric Press.

Levine, S. B. (2003a). What patients mean by love, intimacy, and sexual desire. In S. B. Levine, C. B. Risen & S. E. Althof (Eds.), *The handbook of clinical sexuality for mental health professionals* (pp. 21–36). New York: Brunner-Routledge.

Levine, S. B. (2003b). The nature of sexual desire: A clinician's perspective. *Archives of Sexual Behavior*, 32(3), 279–285.

Levine, S. B. (2005). A reintroduction to clinical sexuality. *Focus: A Journal of Lifelong Learning in Psychiatry*, 3(4), 526–531.

Levine, S. B. (2006). PDE5 inhibitors and psychiatry. *Journal of Clinical Practice in Psychiatry*, 12(1), 1–6.

Levine, S. B., & Risen, C. B. (in press). Professionals who are accused of sexual boundary violations. In F. M. Saleh, A. J. Grudzinskas, & J. M. Bradford (Eds.), *Sex offenders: Identification, risk assessment, treatment, and legal issues.* Oxford: Oxford University Press.

Levine, S. B., & Stagno, S. (2001). Informed consent for case reports: The ethical dilemma between right to privacy and pedogogical freedom. *Journal of Psychotherapy: Research and Practice,* 10(3), 193–201.

Lewis, C. S. (1960). *The four loves.* New York: Harcourt Brace.

Lieberman, J. A., Stroup, T. S., McEvoy, J., Swartz, M. S., Rosenhack, R. A., Perkins, D. O. et al. (2005). Effectiveness of antipsychotic drugs in patients with chronic schizophrenia. *New England Journal of Medicine,* 353, 1209–1223.

Lusterman, D. D. (1998). *Infidelity: A survival guide.* Oakland, CA: New Harbinger.

Masters, W. H., & Johnson, V. (1970). *Human sexual inadequacy.* Boston: Little, Brown.

McCarthy, B. W. (1999). Relapse prevention strategies and techniques for inhibited sexual desire. *Journal of Sexual and Marital Therapy,* 25, 297–303.

McCarthy, B. W., & McCarthy, E. (2003). *Rekindling desire: A step-by-step program to help low-sex and no-sex marriages.* New York: Brunner-Routledge.

Meston, C. M., & Frohlich, P. F. (2000). The neurobiology of sexual function. *Archives of General Psychiatry,* 57(11), 1012–1030.

Mitchell, S. (2002). *Can love last? The fate of romance over time.* New York: W. W. Norton.

Morgan, D. H. J. (2004). The sociological significance of affairs. In J. Duncombe, K. Harrison, G. Allan, & D. Marsden (Eds.), *The state of affairs; Explorations in infidelity and commitment* (pp. 15–34). Mahwah, NJ: Erlbaum.

Moultrup, D. J. (1990). *Husbands, wives, and lovers: The emotional system of the extramarital affair.* New York: Guilford.

North American Menopause Society. (2005). The role of testosterone therapy in postmenopausal women: Position statement of the North American Menopause Society. *Menopause,* 12, 497–511.

Okabe, K., & Mishima, N. (2004). Frequency of marital intercourse among patients with psychiatric and psychosomatic disorders in Japan. *Journal of Sex and Marital Therapy,* 30(3), 3–11.

O'Neill, N., & O'Neill, G. (1972). *Open marriage.* New York: Avon.

Person, E. S., Terestman, N., Myers, W. A., Goldberg, E. L., & Salvadori, C. (1989). Gender differences in sexual behavior and fantasies in a college population. *Journal of Sex and Marital Therapy,* 15(3), 187–198.

Philips, A. (1994). *On flirtation.* Cambridge, MA: Harvard University Press.

Pittman, F. (1989). *Private lies: Infidelity and the betrayal of intimacy.* New York: W. W. Norton.

Plato. (1956). *The symposium.* New York: Tudor.

Puchalski, C. M. (2002, September 17, 2002). Forgiveness: Spiritual and medical implications. *Yale Journal of Humanities in Medicine.* Retrieved from http://info.med.yale.edu/intmed/hummed/yjhm/spirit/forgiveness/cpuchalski.htm.

Randall, H. E., & Byers, E. S. (2003). What is sex? Students' definition of having sex, sexual partners, and unfaithful behaviors. *Canadian Journal of Human Sexuality,* 12 (2), 87–96.

Regan, P. C. (2000). Love relationships. In F. Muscarella (Ed.), *Psychological perspectives on human sexuality* (pp. 232–282). New York: Wiley.

Regan, P. C., & Atkins, L. (2006). Sex differences and similarities in frequency and intensity of sexual desire. *Social Behavior and Personality: An International Journal,* 34(1), 95–101.

Roberts, L. W., & Dyer, R. (2004). *Ethics in mental health.* Washington, D.C.: American Psychiatric Press.

Roisman, G. I., Collins, W. A., Sroufe, L. A., & Egeland, B. (2005). Predictors of young adults' representations of and behavior in their current romantic relationship: Prospective tests of the prototype hypothesis. *Attachment and Human Development,* 7(2), 105–121.

Rosen, R. C., Riley, A., Wagner, G., Osterloh, I. H., Kirkpatrick, J., & Mishra, A. (1997). The International Index of Erectile Dysfunction (IIEF): A multidimensional scale for assessment of erectile dysfunction. *Urology,* 49, 822–830.

Rowland, D. L., Incrocci, L., & Slob, A. K. (2005). Aging and sexual response in the laboratory in patients with erectile dysfunction. *Journal of Sex and Marital Therapy,* 31(5), 399–407.

Rush, A. J., Trivedi, M. H., Wisniewski, S. R. et al. (2006). Bupropion-SR, sertraline, or venlafaxine-XR after failure of SSRIs for depression. *The New England Journal of Medicine,* 354(12), 1231–1242.

Sager, C. J., Kaplan, H. S., Gundlach, R. H., Kremer, M., Lenz, R., & Royce, J. R. (1971). Marital contracts. *Family Process,* 10(3), 310.

Scheinkman, M. (2005). Beyond the trauma of betrayal: Reconsidering affairs in couples therapy. *Family Process,* 44(2), 227–244.

Schiavi, R. C., Schreiner-Engel, P., Mandeli, J., Schanzer, H., & Cohen, E. (1990). Healthy aging and male sexual function. *American Journal of Psychiatry,* 147(6), 766–771.

Schiavi, R. C., & Segraves, R. T. (1995). The biology of sexual function. *Psychiatric Clinics of North America,* 18(1), 17–23.

Schnarch, D. M. (2000). Desire problems: A systemic perspective. In Rosen, R. C. Lieblum S R (Ed.), *Principles and practice of sex therapy* (3rd ed., pp. 17–56). New York: Guilford Press.

Schover, L. & Jensen, S. B. (1988). *Sexuality and Chronic Illness*. A comprehensive approach. New York: Guilford Press.

Shifren, J. L., Braunstein, G. D., Simon, J. A. , Casson, P. R., Buster, J. E., Redmond, G. P. et al. (2000). Transdermal testosterone treatment in women with impaired sexual function after oophorectomy. *New England Journal of Medicine*, 343(10), 682–688.

Simon, J., Braunstein, G., Nachtigall, L. et al. (2005). Testosterone patch increases sexual activity and desire in surgically menopausal women with hypoactive sexual desire disorder. *The Journal of Clinical Endocrinology and Metabolism*, 90(9), 5226–5233.

Singer, I. (1984). *The nature of love: Vol. 2. Courtly and romantic*. Chicago: University of Chicago Press.

Slater, L. (2006, February). True love: The chemical reaction. *National Geographic*, 209, 32–49.

Sprecher, S. (1994). Two sides to the breakup of dating relationships. *Personal Relationships*, 1, 199–222.

Stein, D. J., Black, D. W., Shapira, N. A., & Spitzer, R. L. (2001). Hypersexual disorder and preoccupation with Internet pornography. *American Journal of Psychiatry*, 158, 1590–1594.

Sternberg, R. J. (1988). *A triangular theory of love: Intimacy, passion, and commitment*. New York: Basic Books.

Stoller, R. J. (1975). *Perversion: The erotic form of hatred*. New York: Pantheon.

Strean, H. (1980). *The extramarital affair*. New York: Free Press.

Tennov, D. (1979). *Love and limerance: The experience of being in love in New York*. New York: Stein & Day.

Thornton, A., & Young-DeMarco, L. (2001). Four decades of trends in attitudes towards family issues in the United States: The 1960s through the 1990s. *Journal of Marriage and the Family*, 63, 1009–1037.

Tolman, D. L. (2002). Dilemmas of desire: *Teenage girls talk about sexuality*. Cambridge, MA: Harvard University Press.

Trivedi, M. H., Rush, A. J., Wisniewski, S. R., Nierenberg, A. A., Warden, D., Ritz, L. et al. (2006). Outcomes with citalopram for depression using measurement-based care in STAR*-D: implications for clinical practice. *American Journal of Psychiatry*, 163(1), 28–40.

Viorst, J. (1986). Love and hate in the married state. In J. Viorst (Ed.), *Necessary losses* (pp. 185–204). New York: Free Press.

Watts, S., & Stenner, P. (2005). The subjective experience of partnership love: A Q methodology. *British Journal of Social Psychology*, 44, 85–107.

Weeks, G., Gambescia, N., & Jenkins, R. (Eds.). (2003). *Treating infidelity: Therapeutic dilemmas and effective strategies*. New York: W. W. Norton.

Weil, S. M. (2003). The extramarital affair: A language of yearning and loss. *Clinical Social Work,* 31, 51–62.

Weitzman, G. D. (1999). *What psychology professionals should know about polyamory: The lifestyles and mental health concerns of polyamorous individuals.* Retrieved August 22, 2006 from http://www.polyamory.org/~joe/polypaper.htm.

Whitehurst, R. N. (1971). Sexual responses. *Journal of Marriage and the Family,* 33, 683–691.

WHI Writing Group. (2002). Risks and benefits of estrogen plus progesterone in healthy postmenopausal women: Principal results from the Women's Health Initiative randomized controlled trial. *Journal of the American Medical Association,* 288, 321–333.

Wiederman, M. W. (1997). Extramarital sex: Prevalence and correlates in a national survey. *The Journal of Sex Research, 34*(2), 167–174.

Wolpe, D. (2000). *Finding a way to forgive.* Woodstock, VT: Jewish Lights.

Wright, R. (1994). *The Moral Animal: Evolutionary psychology and everyday life.* New York: Vintage Books.

Wynne, L. (1986). The quest for intimacy. *Journal of Marital and Family Therapy,* 12, 383–392.

Index

W

Women, *see also* Gender
   postmenopausal women and,
      92–93
   predictors and, 31–32
   pregnancy and, 86
   psychological intimacy and,
      67–68
Work
   falling in love with patients
      and, 49–50
   love as management process,
      7–8
   professional humility and, 47
   society and expectations, 48
   volatile first sessions and, 42

Y

Youthful romantic ideals, 141
   infidelity and, 141